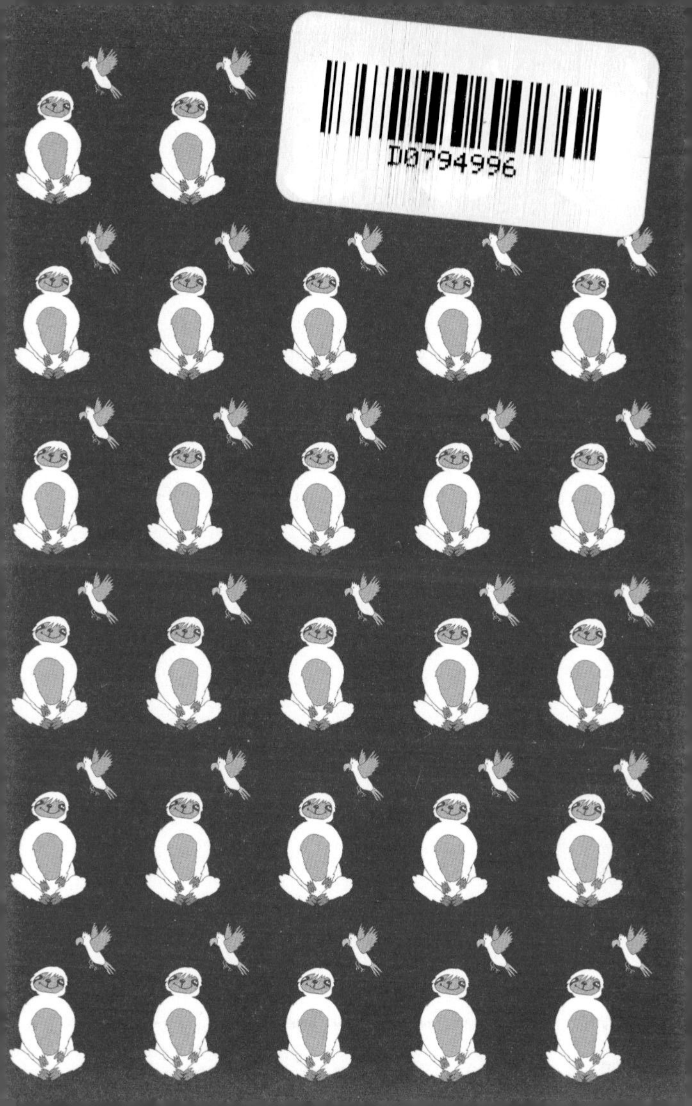

BE A SLOTH

& when in doubt, just chill out

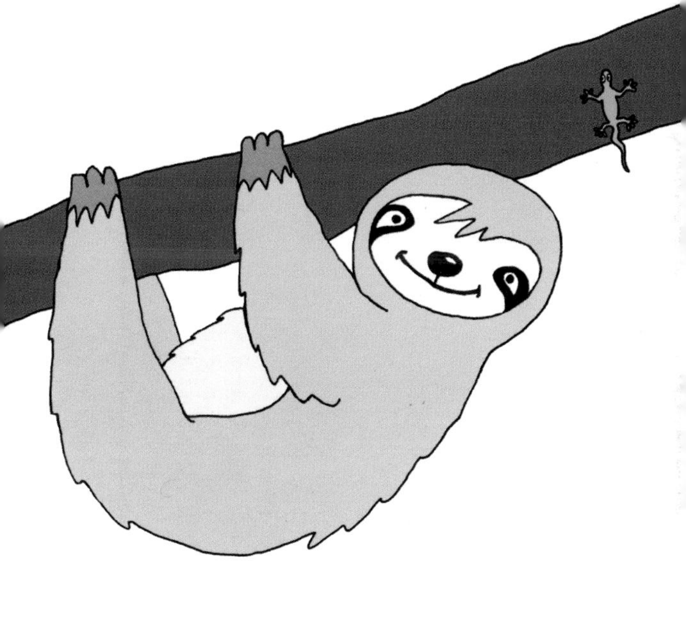

SARAH FORD

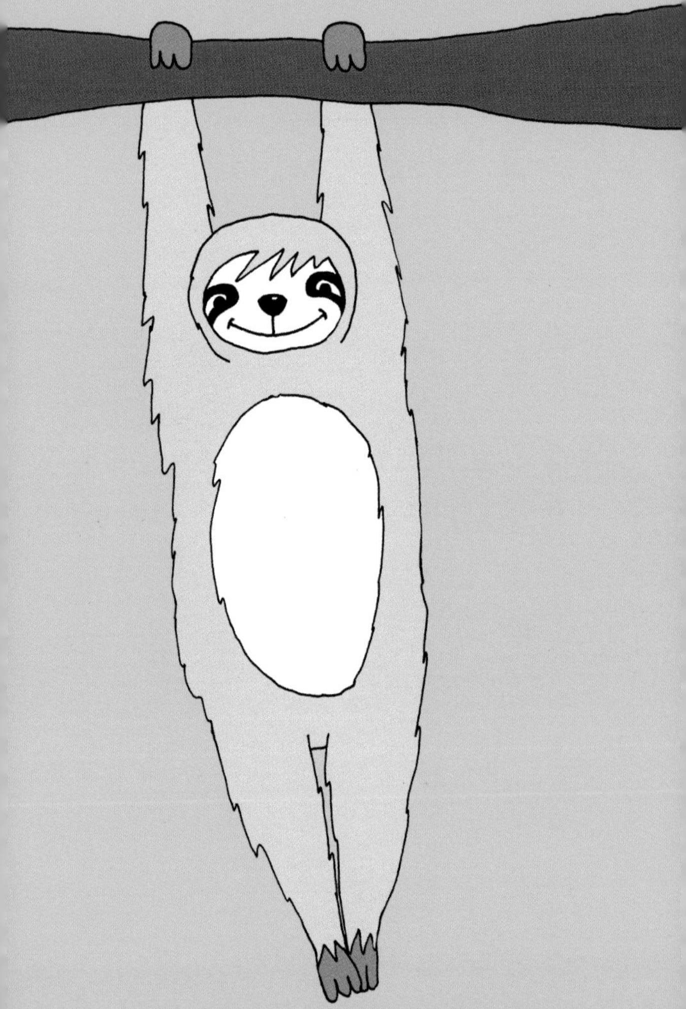

BE A SLOTH

& when in doubt, just chill out

SARAH FORD

ILLUSTRATED BY
ANITA MANGAN

spruce

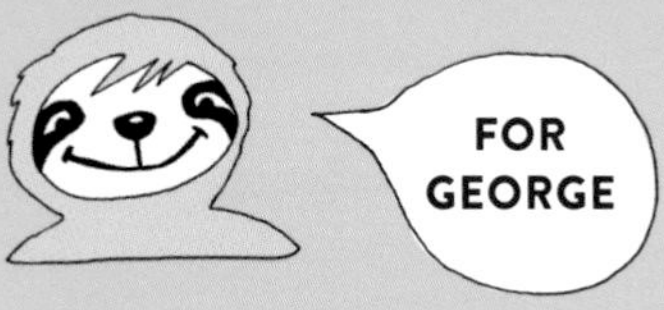
FOR
GEORGE

NOTES

- Contains everything you need to press pause.
- Not suitable for scurrying lizards.
- No age limit (all things are created equal).
- Spread the power of slow.
- To be enjoyed slowly with a cup of tea, preferably after a small nap.

Sloth is always true to himself. He doesn't do exercise but he does look after himself – he eats well, sleeps well and is in tune with his mind and his body in all its hairy entirety.

Sloth isn't afraid of anything or anybody. He seizes life with all claws, but he does it in his own time and in his own way, untouched by outside pressures. He faces life head-on and would never run away... even if he could.

Sloth cares about his environment. He believes in looking after the planet and being at one with everything around him. He knows that the best things in life are free and he places great value on friendship. Always generous and kind, Sloth knows that what goes around comes around... especially the ice-cream truck, which comes around every day at 3.30pm.

Sloth believes in the right to protest and that peaceful negotiation is the way forward. He has no trouble making and standing by his decisions and has no regrets – what's done is done, live for the day, seize it and squeeze it. Above all else, Sloth believes in enjoying the now and embracing whatever the future brings (after a little nap).

SLOTH'S 10 RULES FOR A FINE LIFE

- Enjoy everything that life has to offer (then recover slowly under a big blanket).

- You have the power to be whatever you want to be – don't wait for things to fall into your lap.

- Best foot forward... slow, sure and fearless wins the race.

- Listen to others, then make up your own mind.

- Things will always seem better in the morning, after a sleep.

- Wear your shorts all year round – long trousers are for softies.

- Share your toffees and everyone will like you.

- Be very wary of brightly coloured birds who talk too much and steal your chips.

- Don't let anything go to waste – one person's junk...

- Honour thy parents, always.

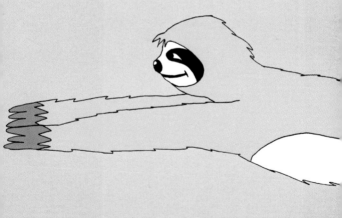

Sloth was very busy,
saving energy.

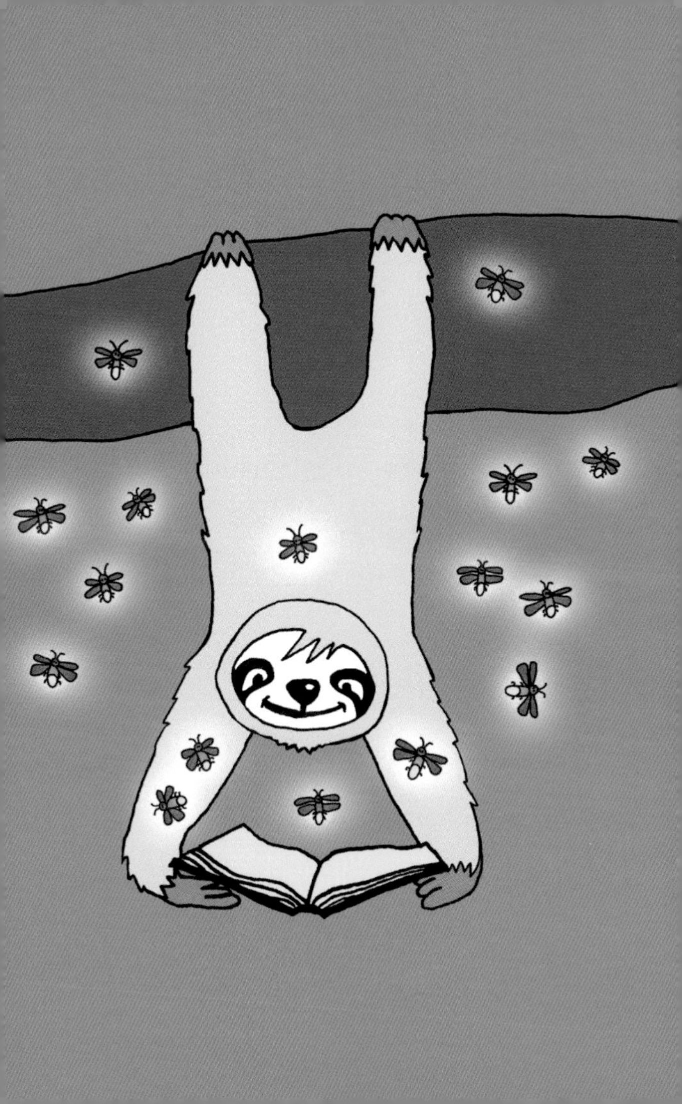

'Do less, achieve more'
was Sloth's mantra
for life.

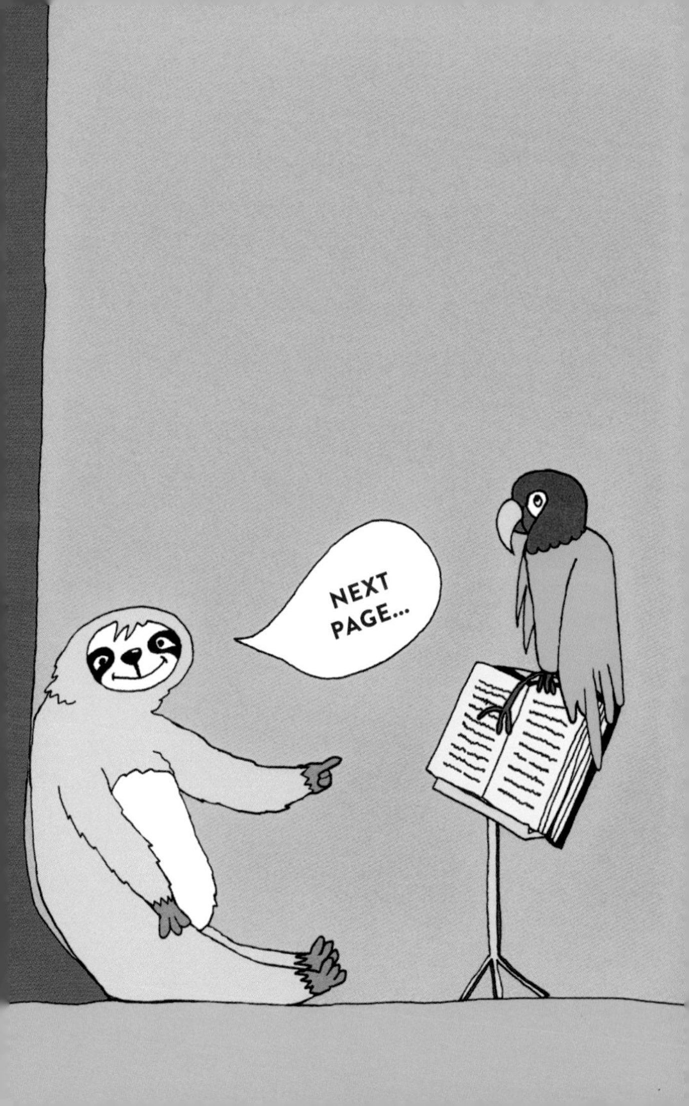
NEXT PAGE...

Sloth was being kind to himself.

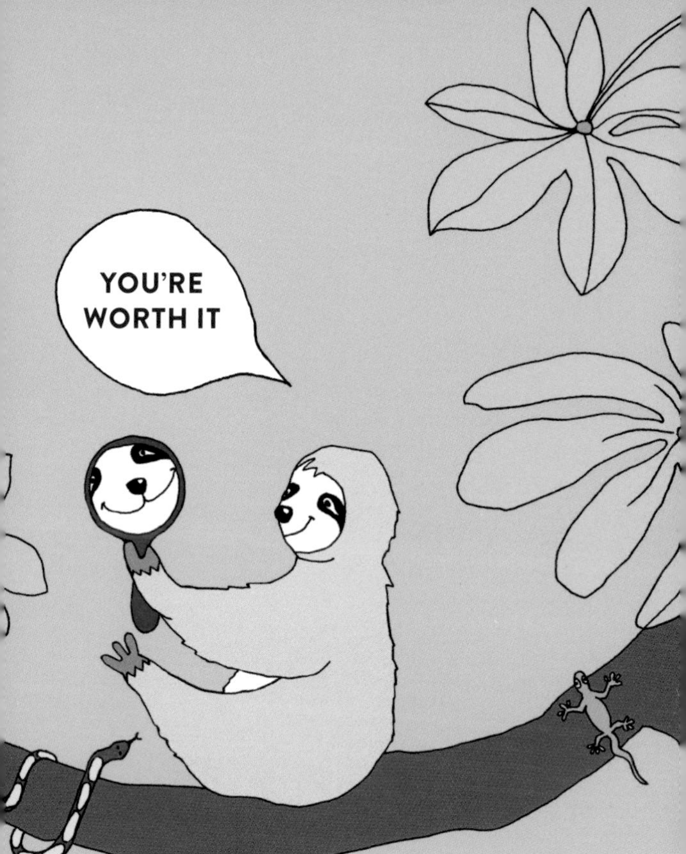
YOU'RE WORTH IT

Sloth had slept for 15 hours and was positively glowing.

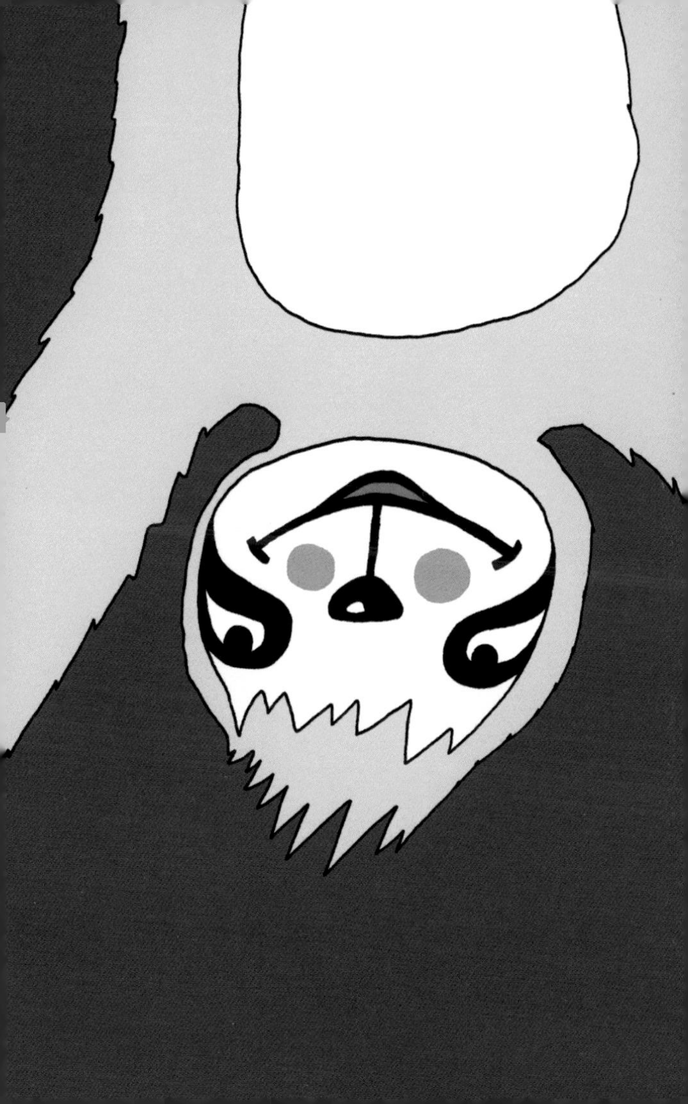

Hanging out with
his pals was Sloth's
favourite thing.

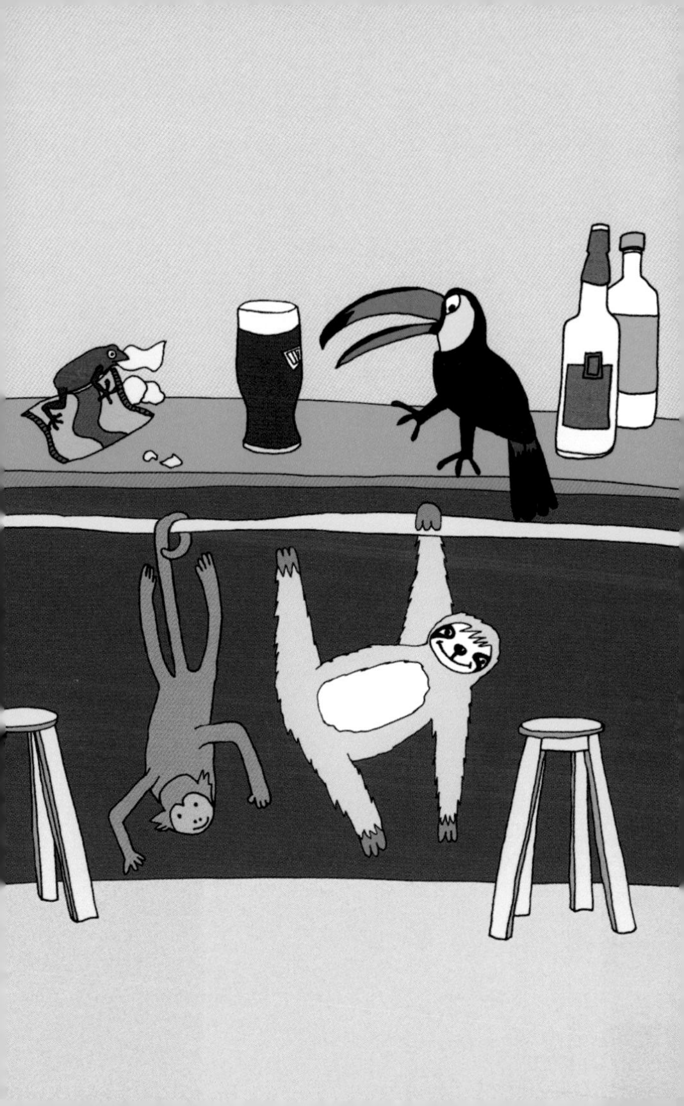

Sloth always felt better
when hugging a tree.

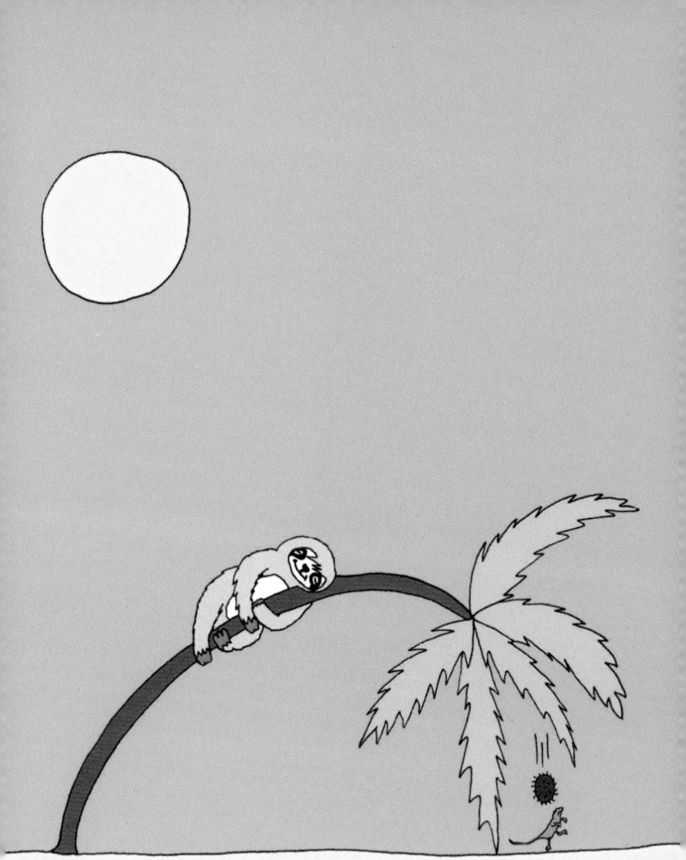

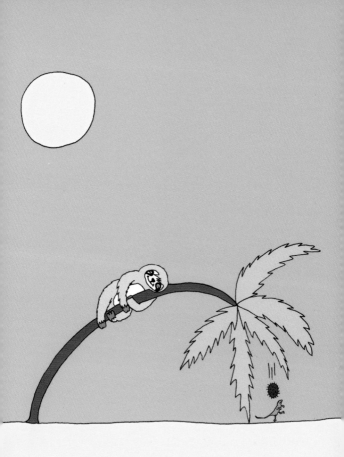

There's always tomorrow,
thought Sloth.

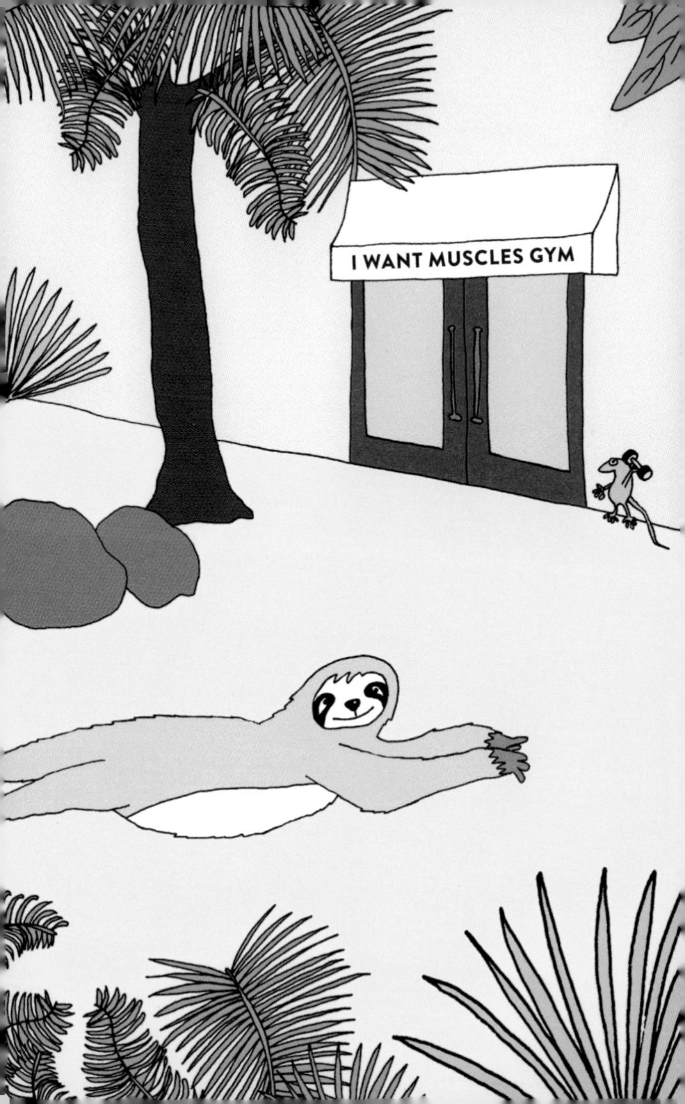
I WANT MUSCLES GYM

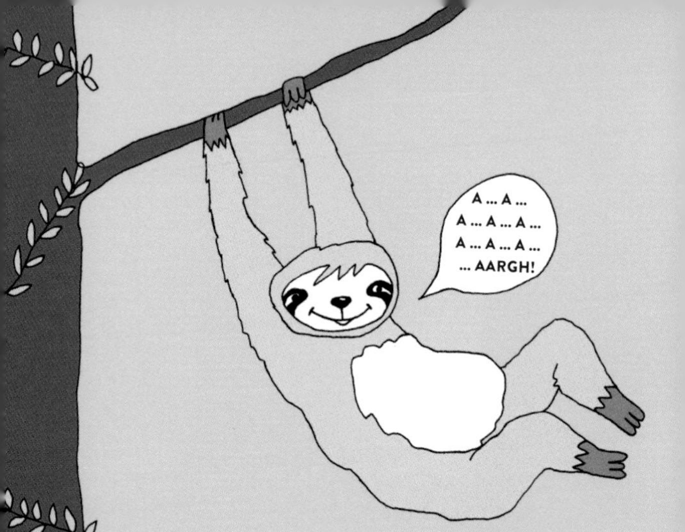
A ... A ...
A ... A ... A ...
A ... A ... A ...
... AARGH!

Sloth was going to
take a leap of faith.

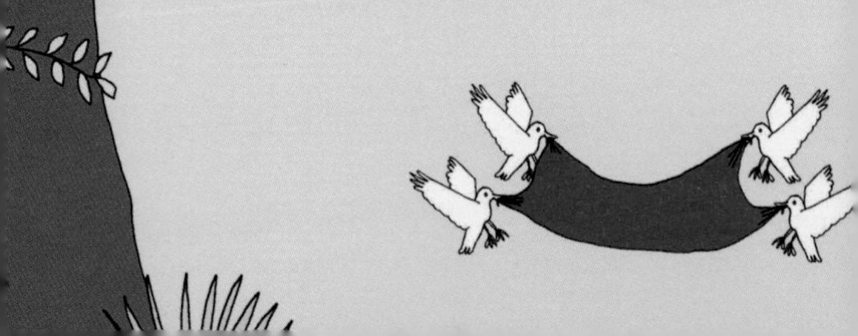

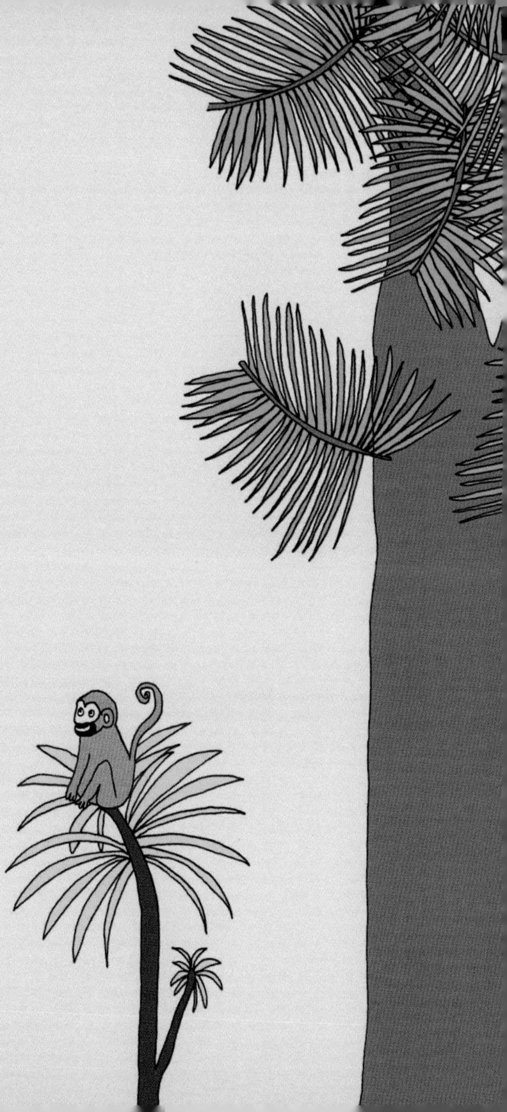

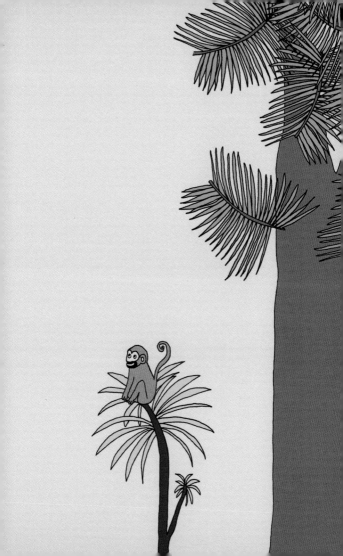

Sloth was forging
his own path.

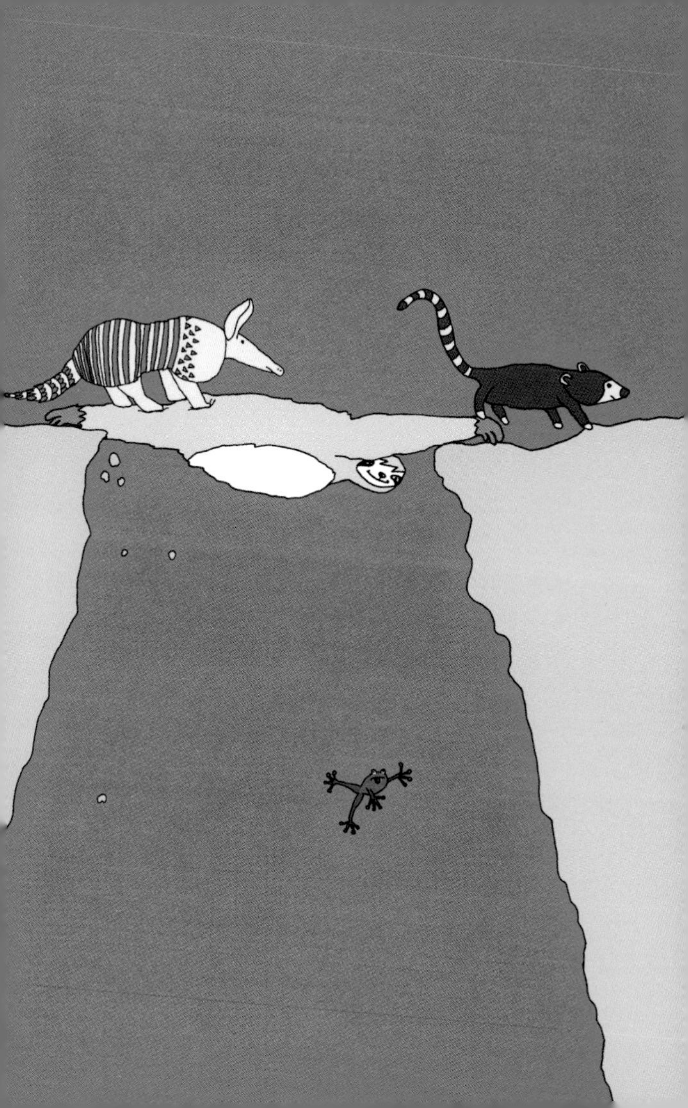

Sloth was making body hair cool again.

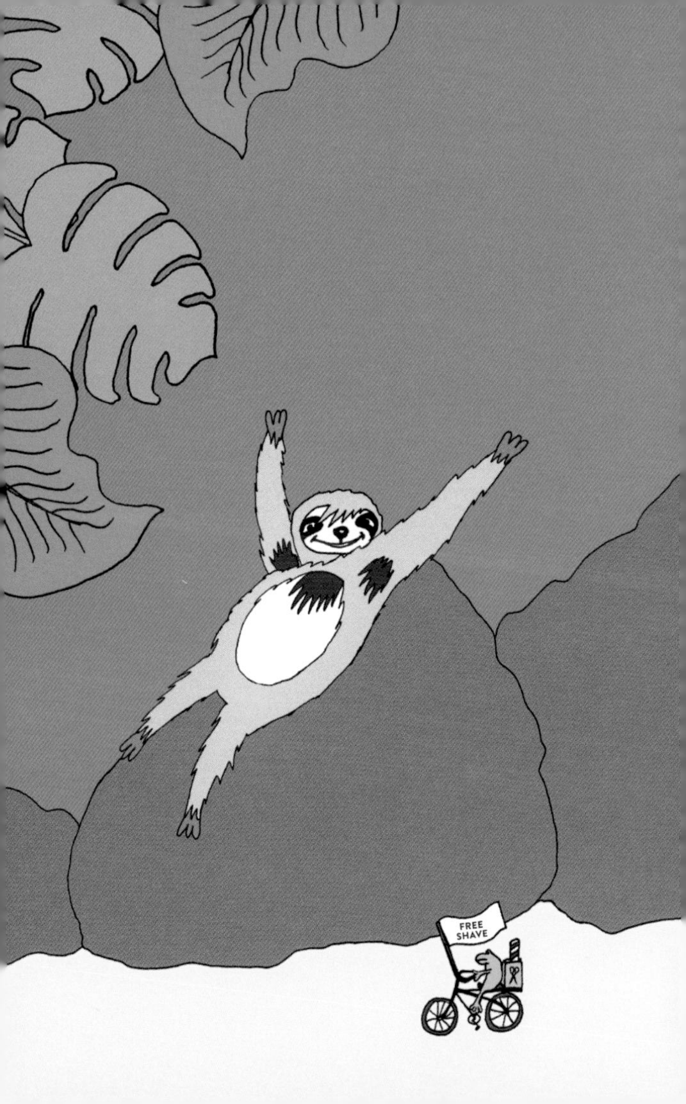
FREE
SHAVE

Sloth was doing
what he loved.

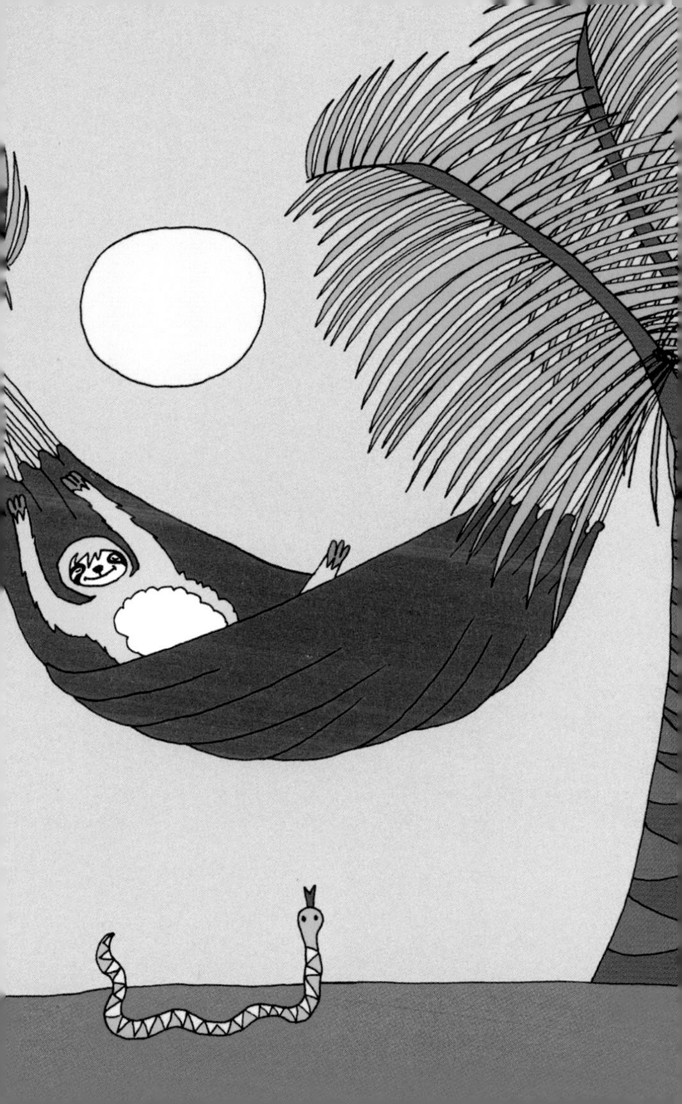

Sloth was
dreaming big.

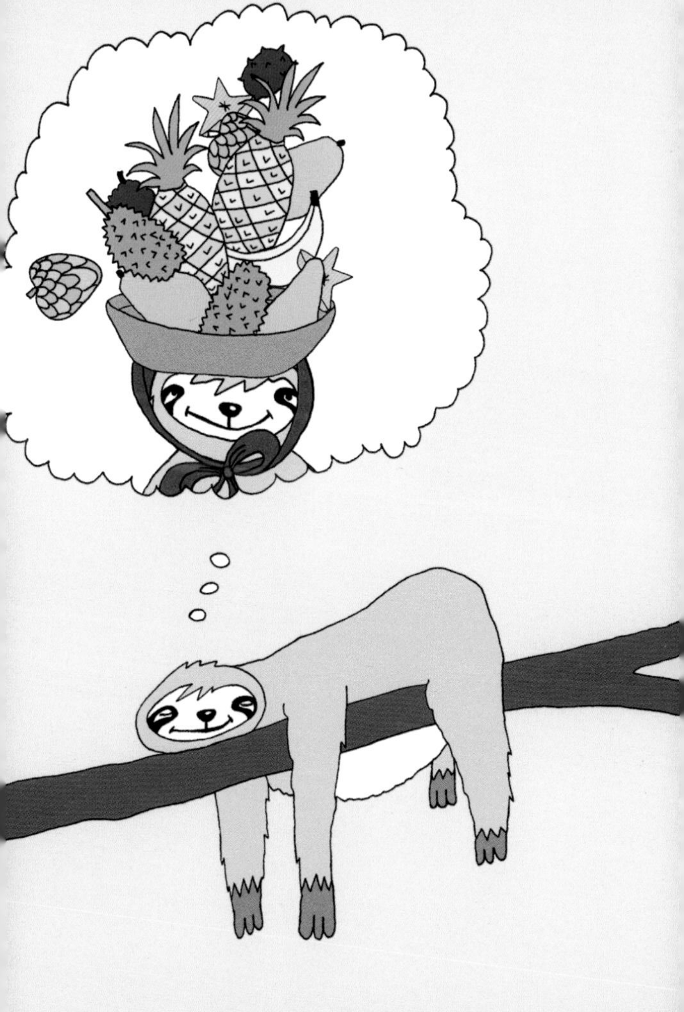

Sloth found sticking
to his vegan diet a
little tricky.

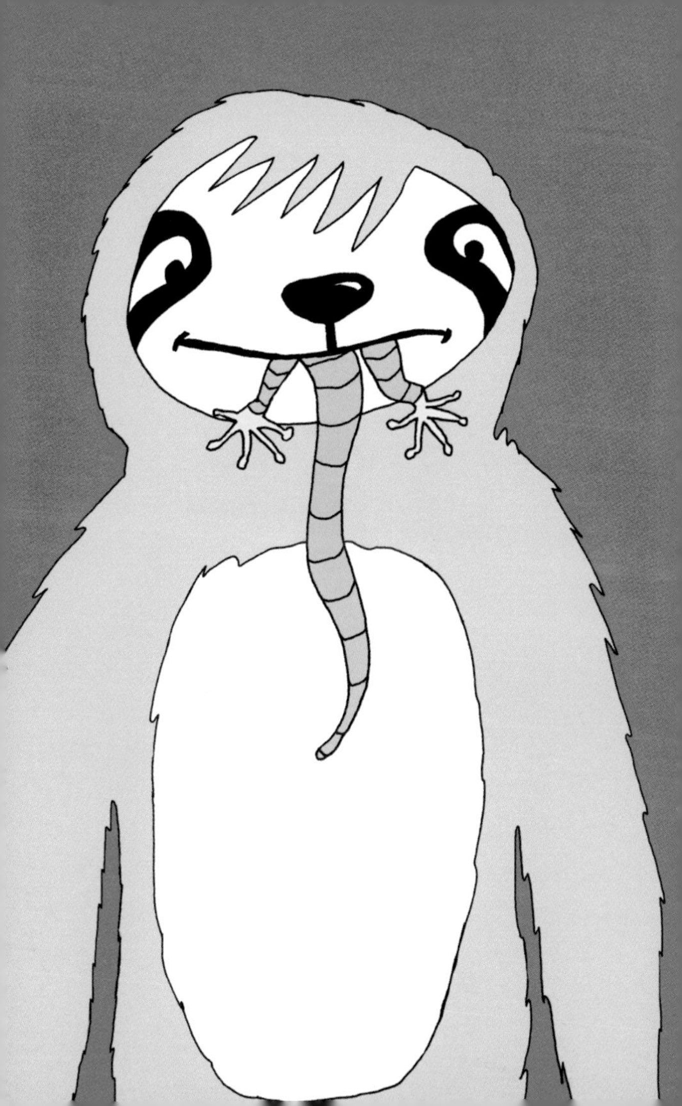

Sloth was committed to living a completely green life.

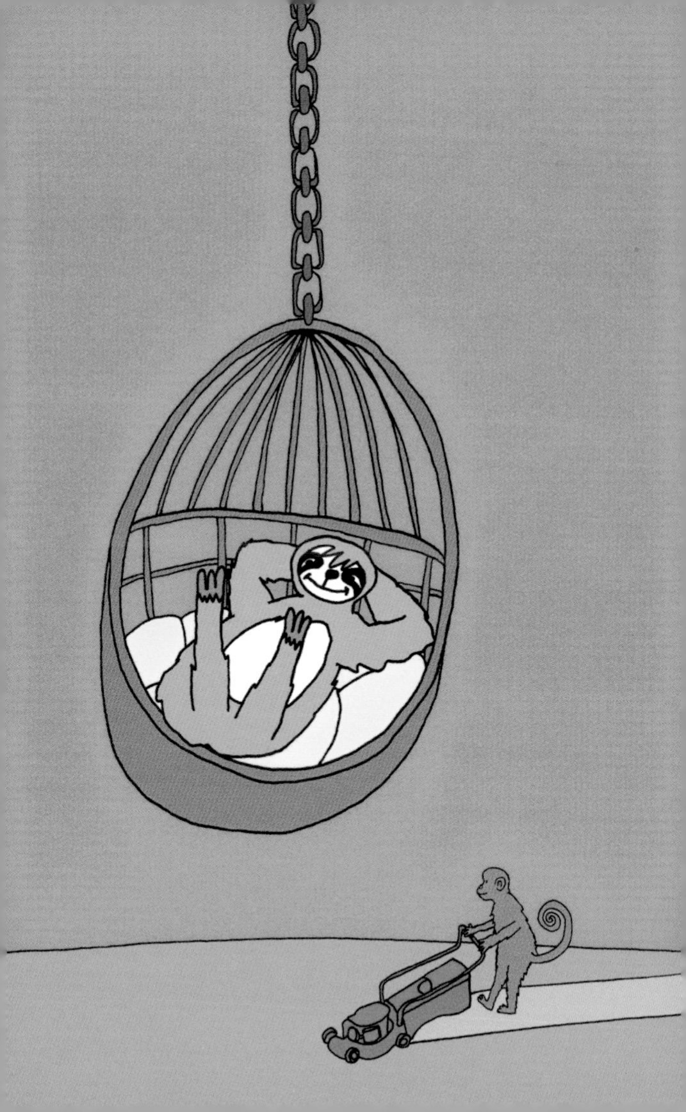

Sloth thought that
sometimes you just
had to go through it.

Time to get a grip,
thought Sloth.

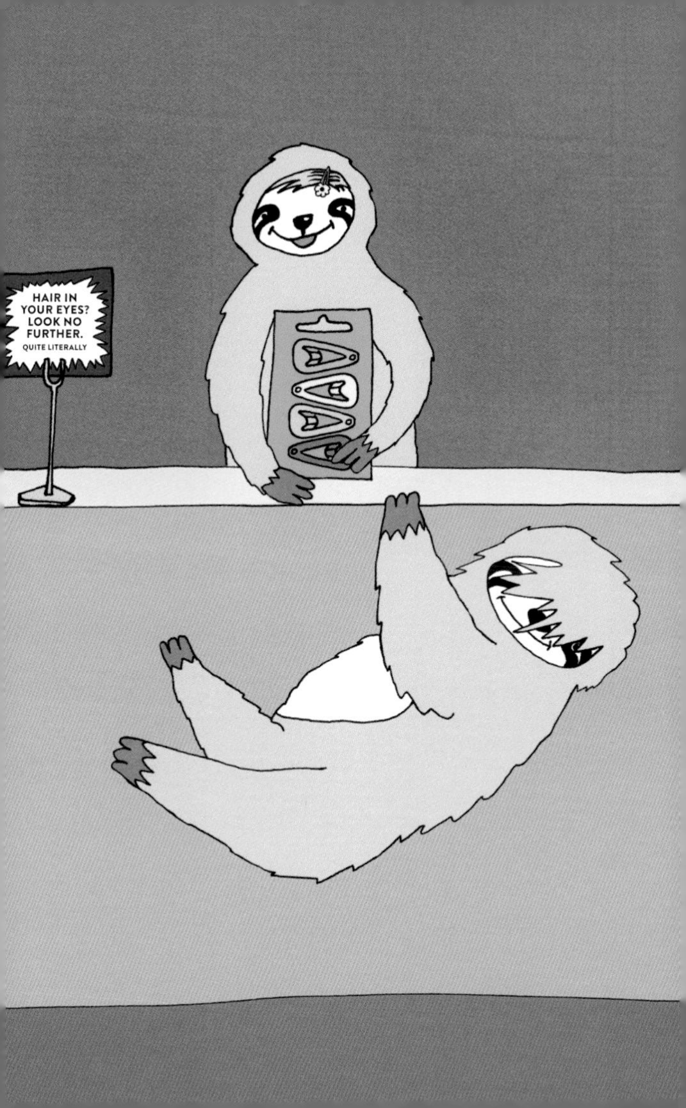
HAIR IN YOUR EYES? LOOK NO FURTHER.
QUITE LITERALLY

Sloth was enjoying
the view.

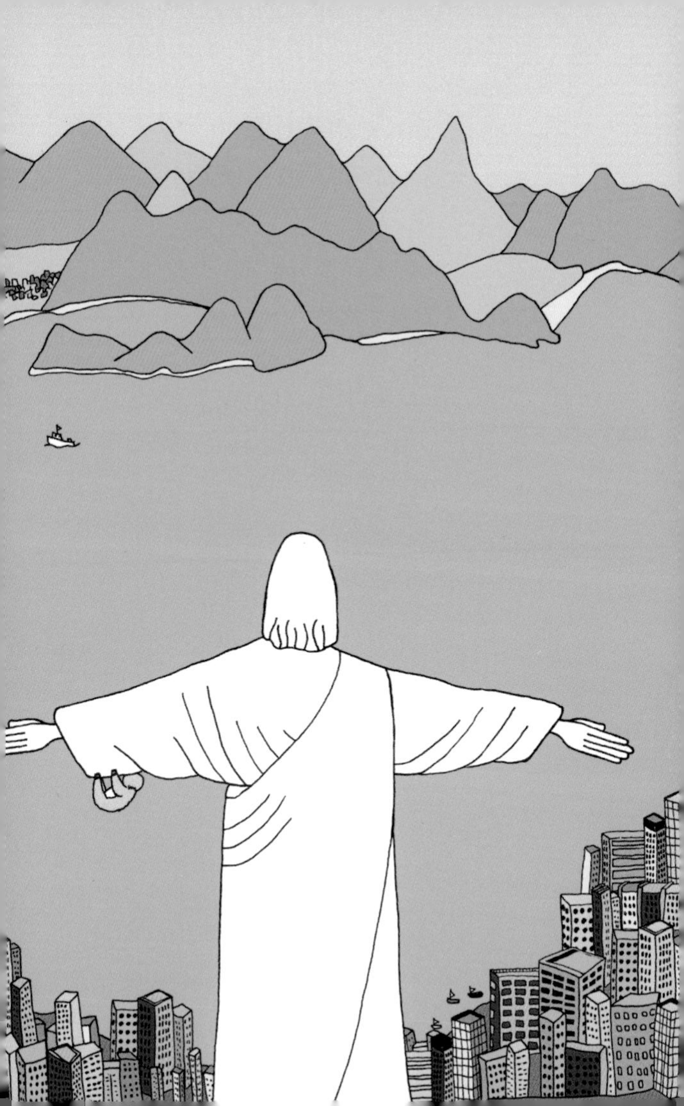

Sloth only used
sustainable products.

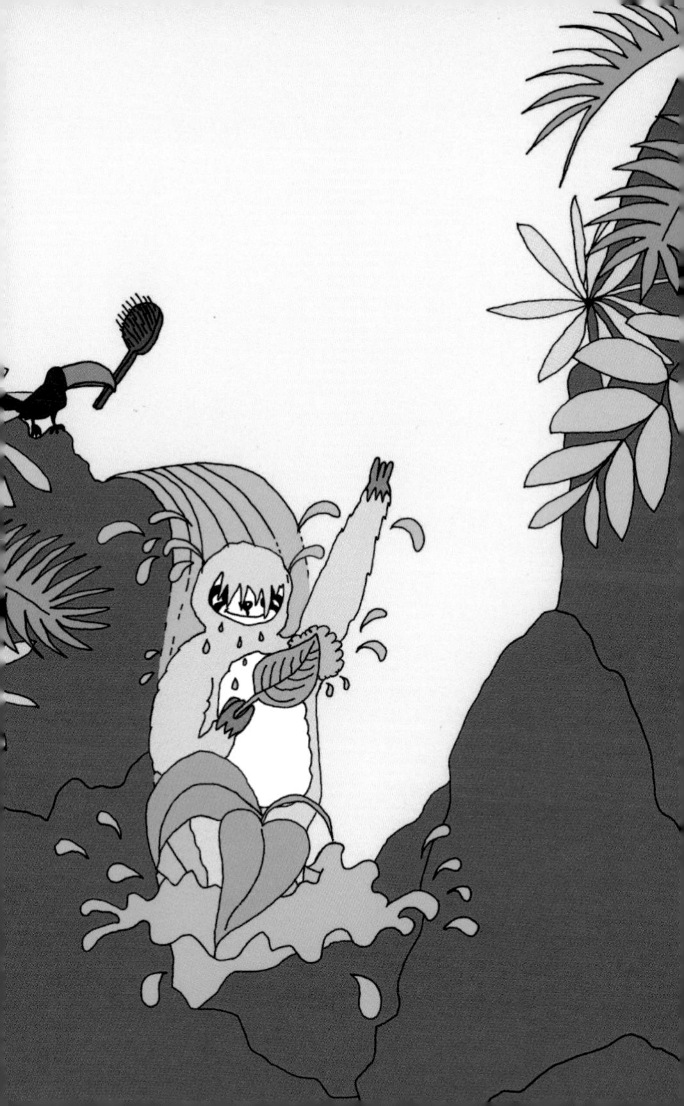

Sloth had tuned
out the chatter.

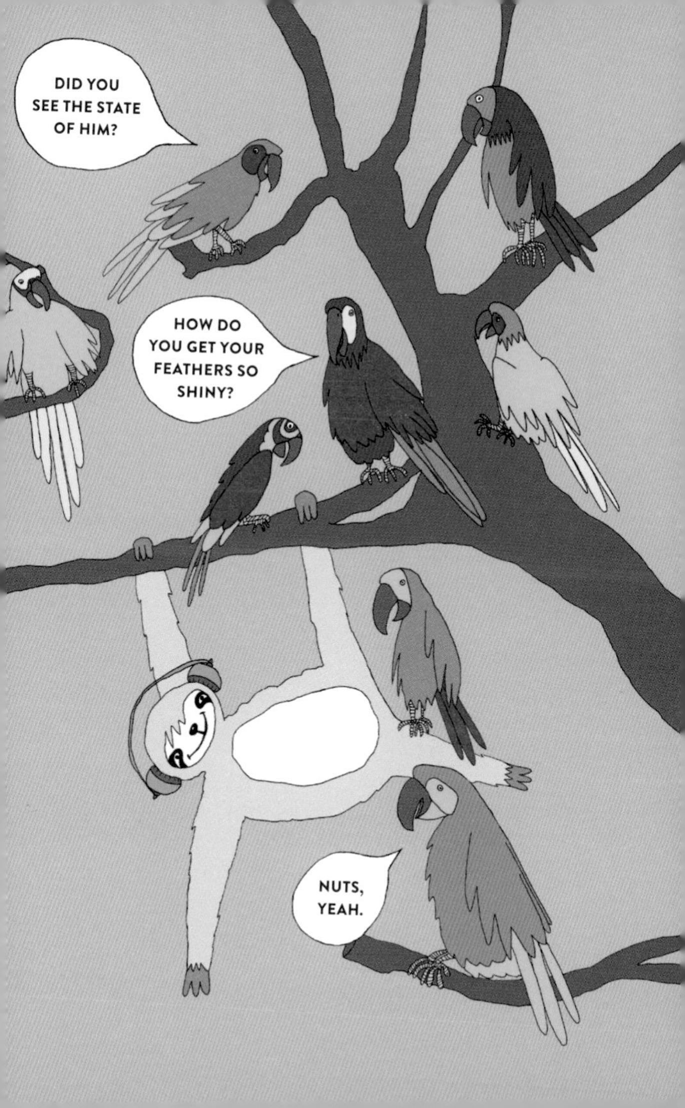
DID YOU SEE THE STATE OF HIM?
HOW DO YOU GET YOUR FEATHERS SO SHINY?
NUTS, YEAH.

Sloth was his
own person.

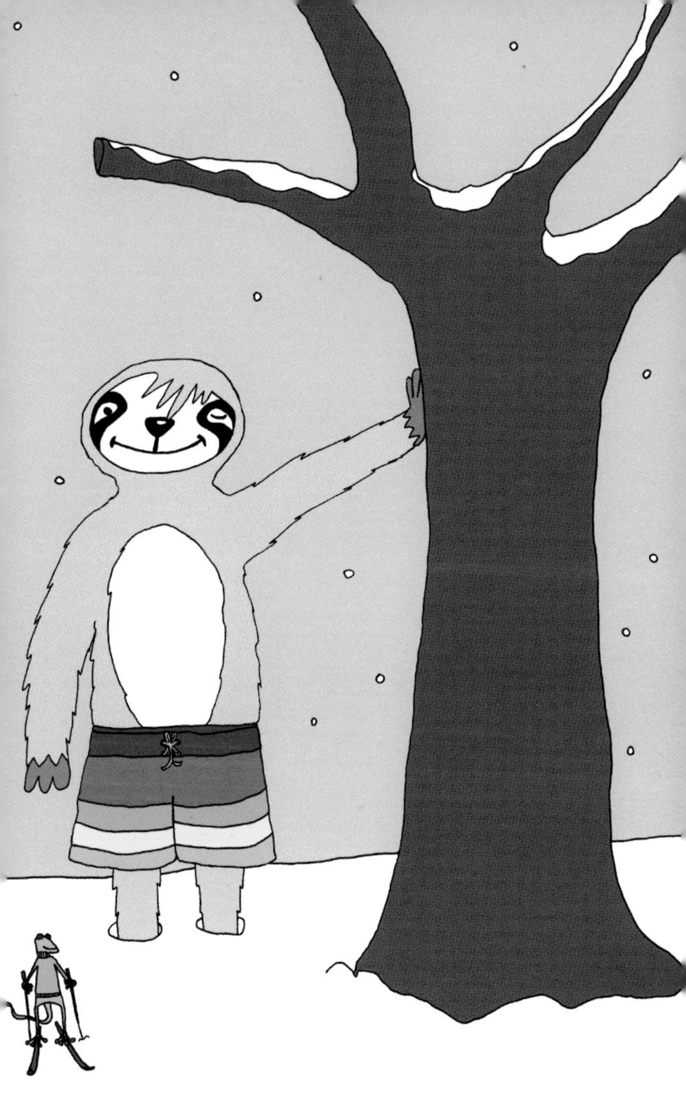

Sloth liked to mix
things up.

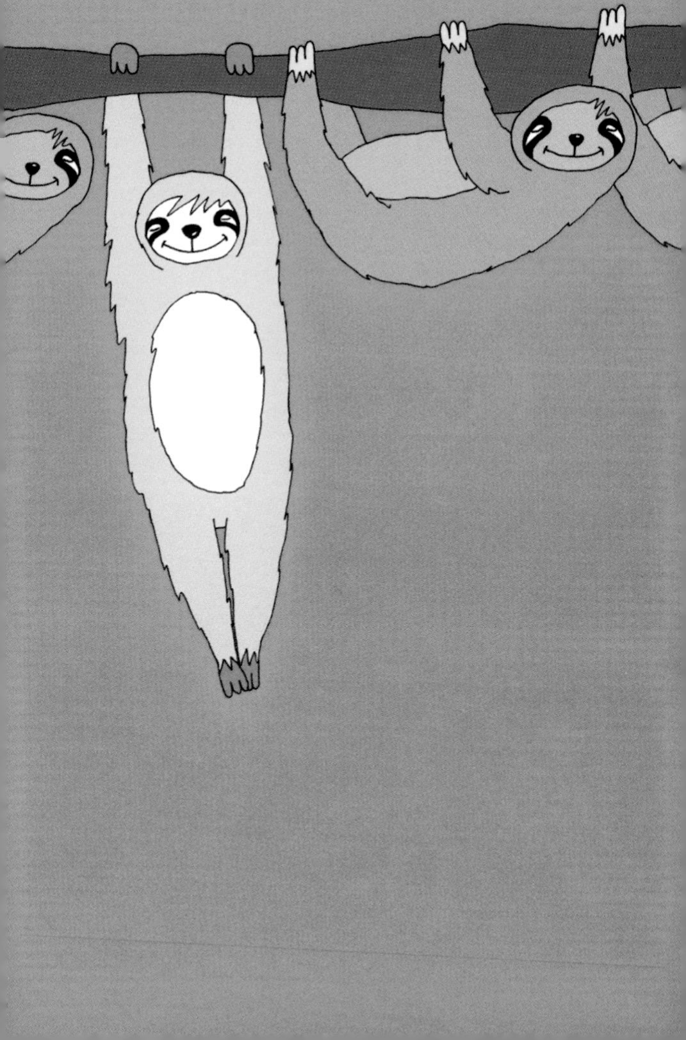

Sloth silenced his inner critic.

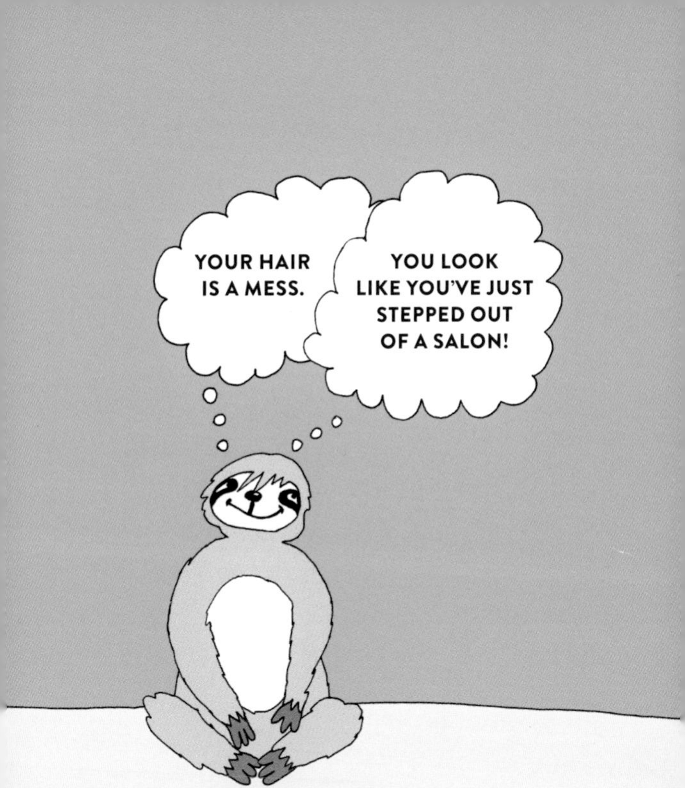
YOUR HAIR IS A MESS.
YOU LOOK LIKE YOU'VE JUST STEPPED OUT OF A SALON!

Sloth thought it
was a mistake to
underestimate the
power of slow.

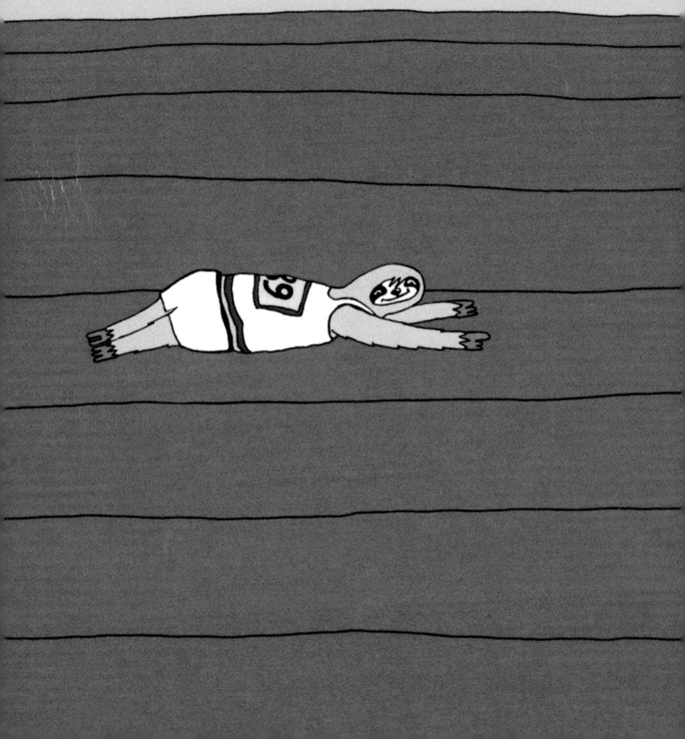

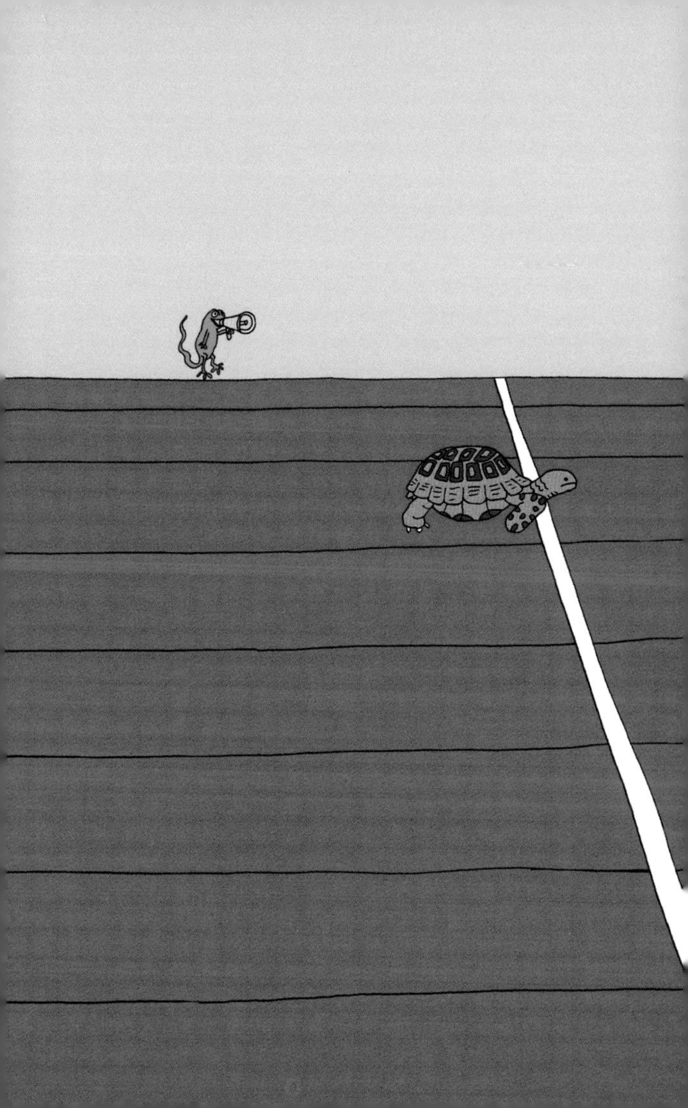

Sloth was a lover,
not a fighter.

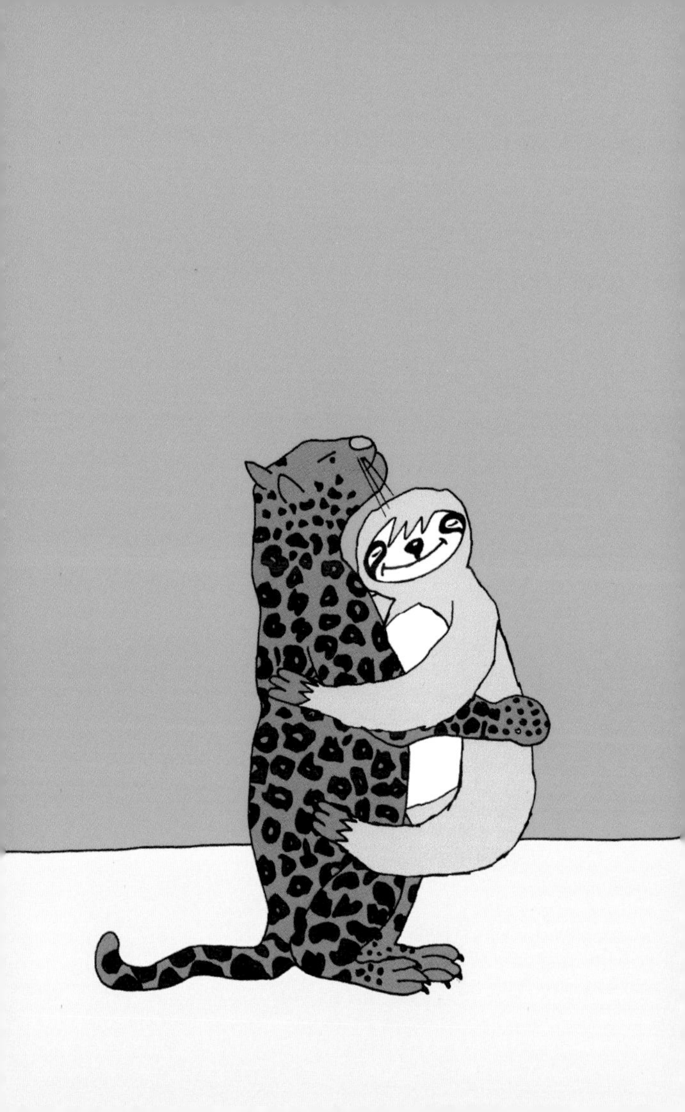

Every now and again,
Sloth liked to turn his
life upside down.

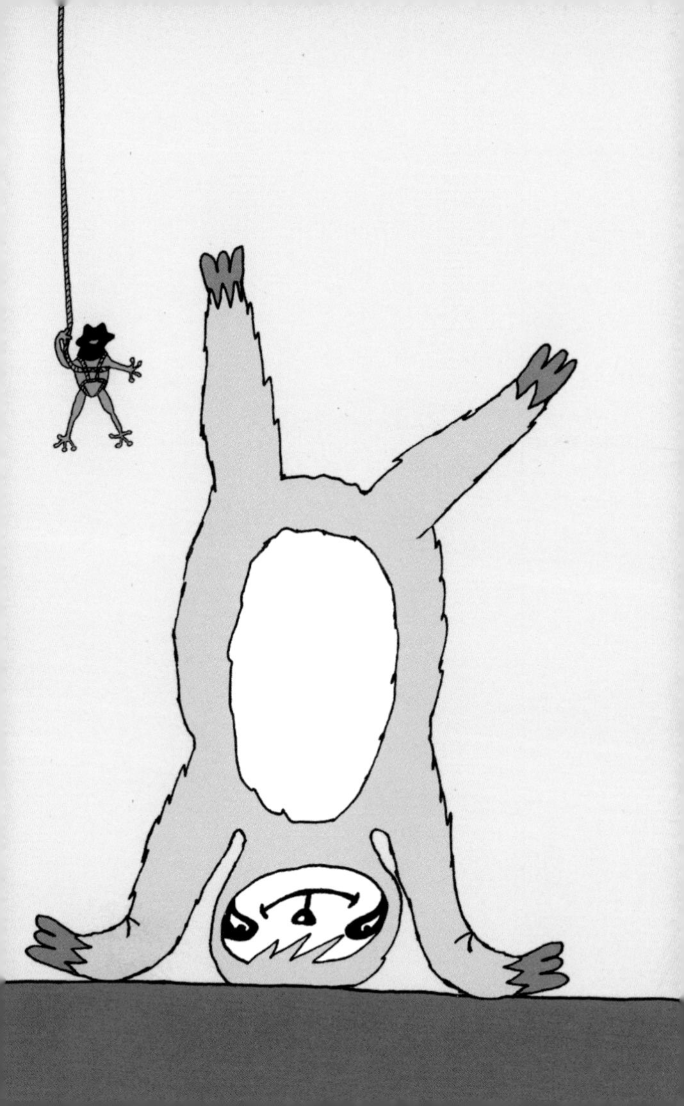

Sloth just let go
of his demons.

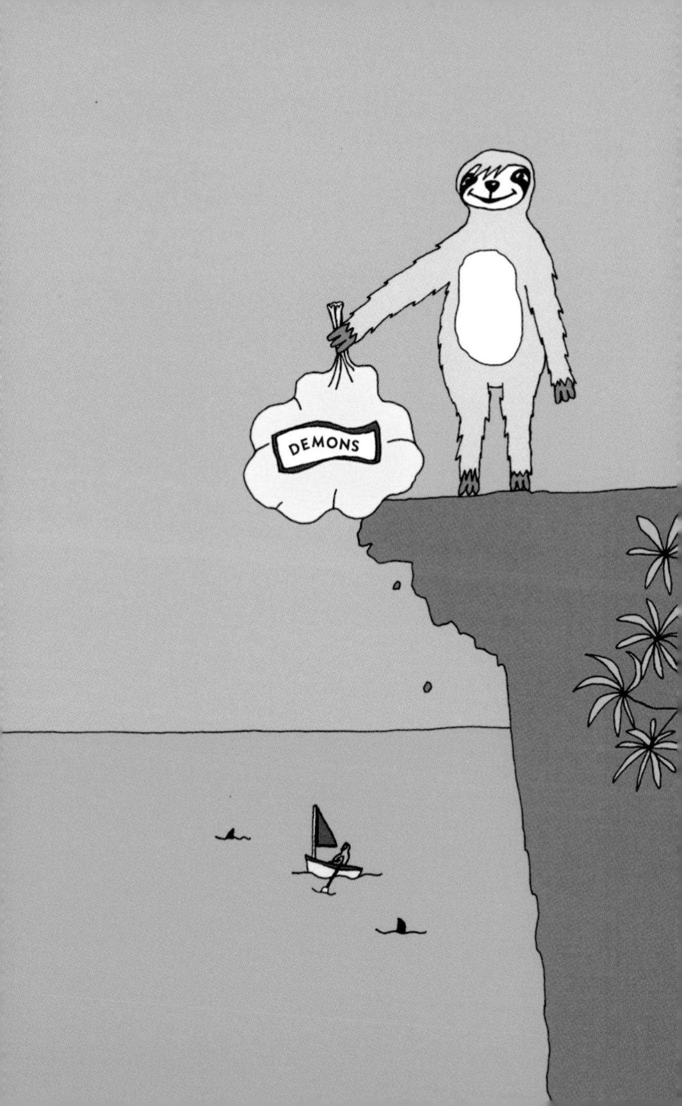
DEMONS

Sloth thought there
was more than one way
to win a debate.

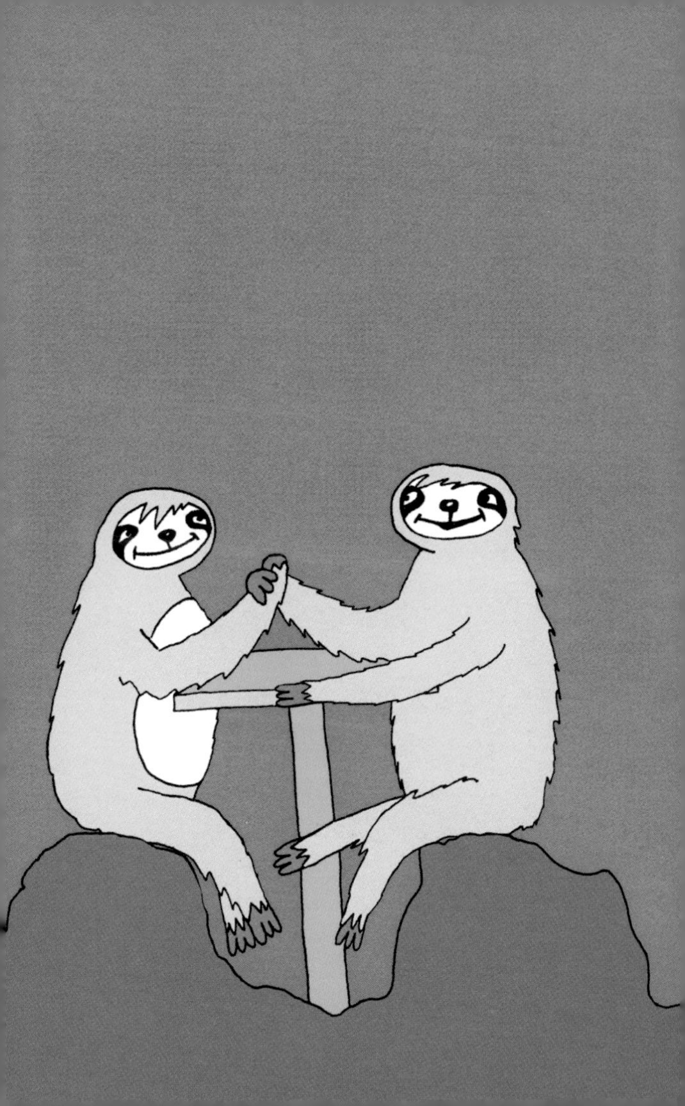

Sloth hoped his persistence would work eventually.

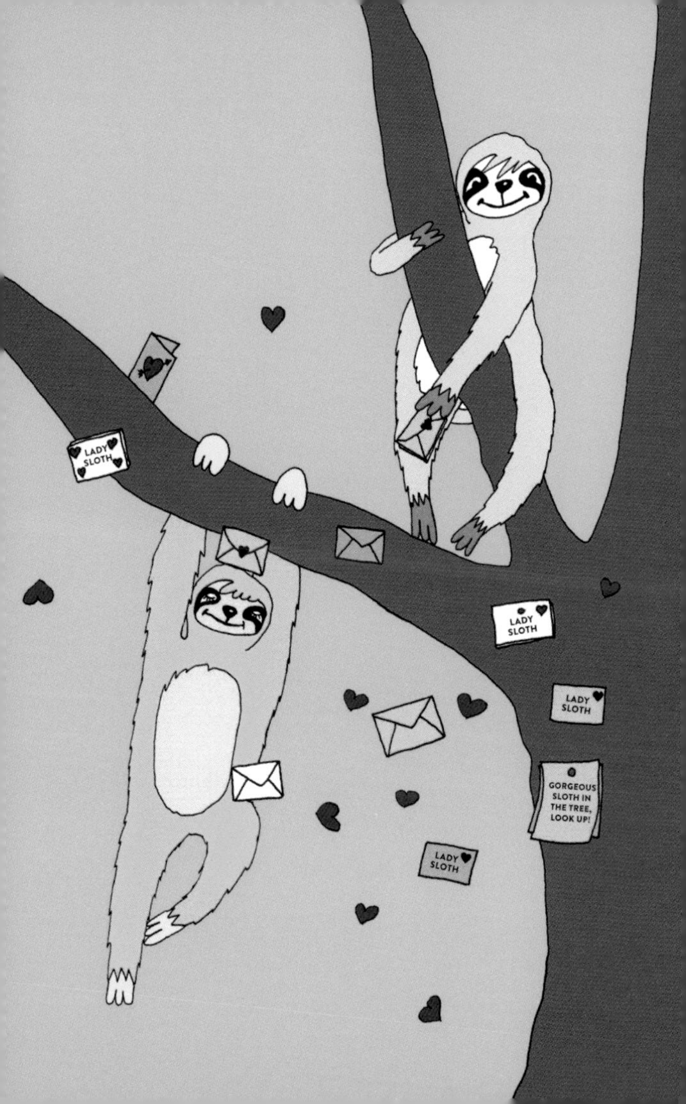
LADY SLOTH
LADY SLOTH
LADY SLOTH
GORGEOUS SLOTH IN THE TREE, LOOK UP!
LADY SLOTH

On paper he was broke
but Sloth still felt rich.

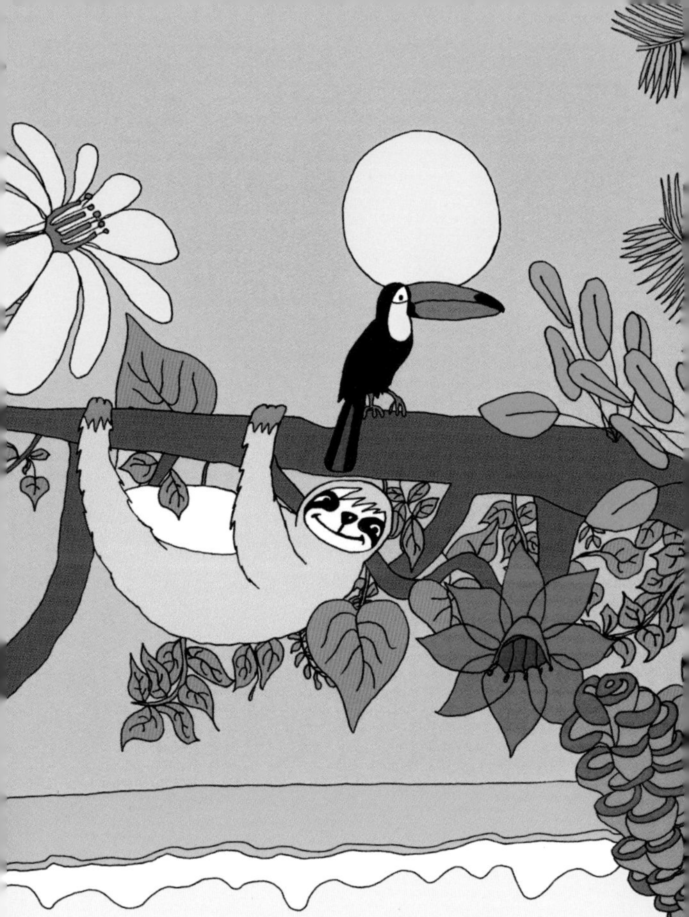

Sloth was looking
forward to going home.

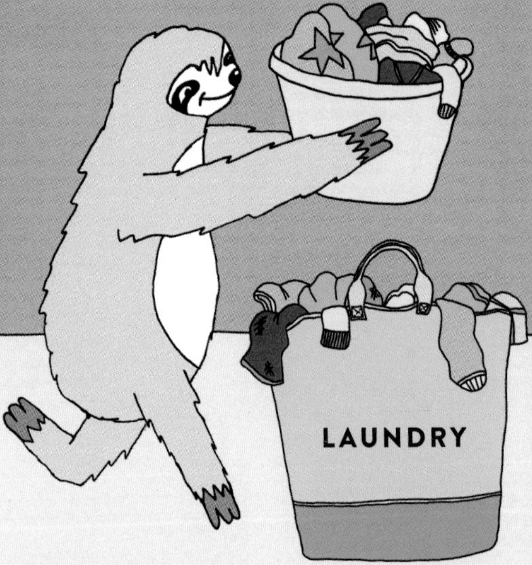
LAUNDRY

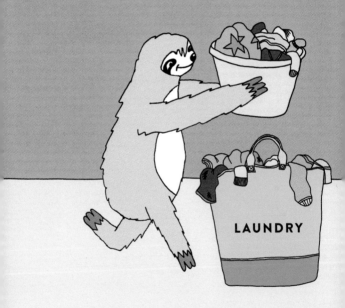

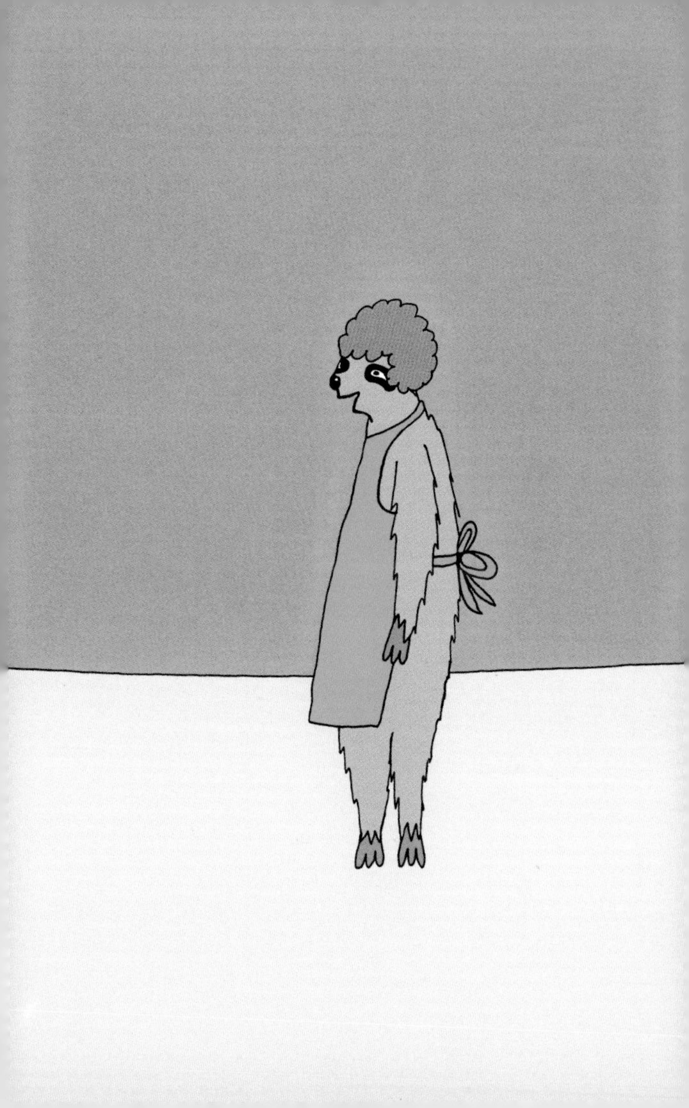

Sloth thought you
could never protest
too much.

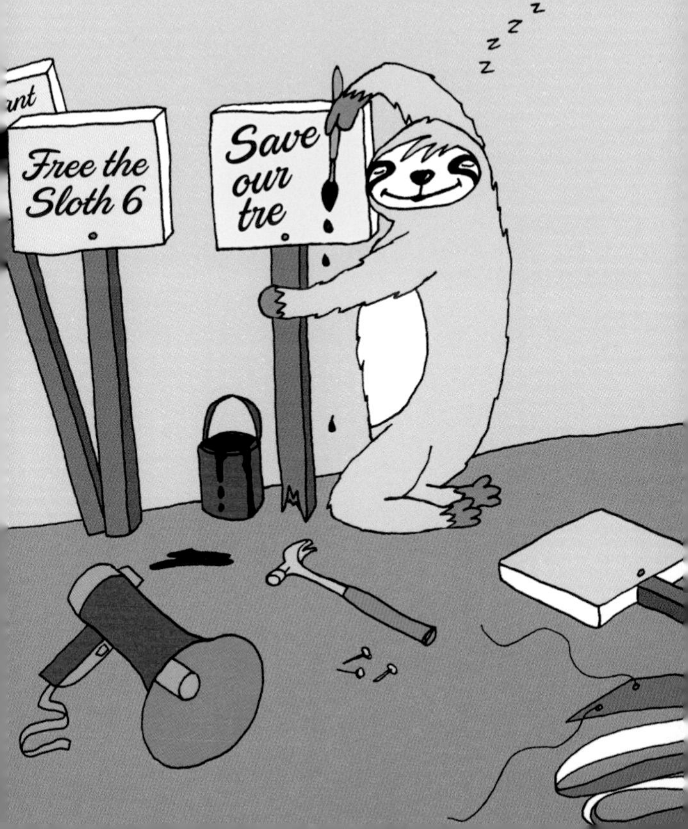

ant
Free the Sloth 6
Save our tre

Sloth liked to try
new things.

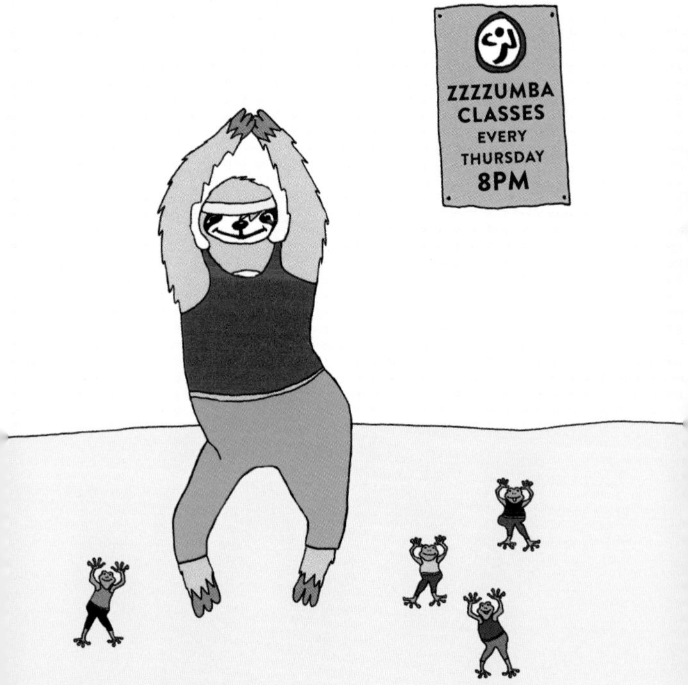
ZZZZUMBA
CLASSES
EVERY
THURSDAY
8PM

Sloth was happy
in his own skin.

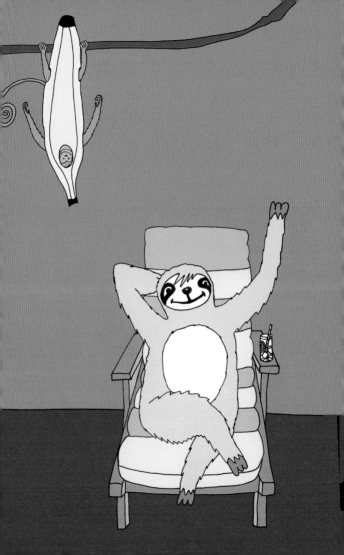

Sloth was playing
to his strengths.

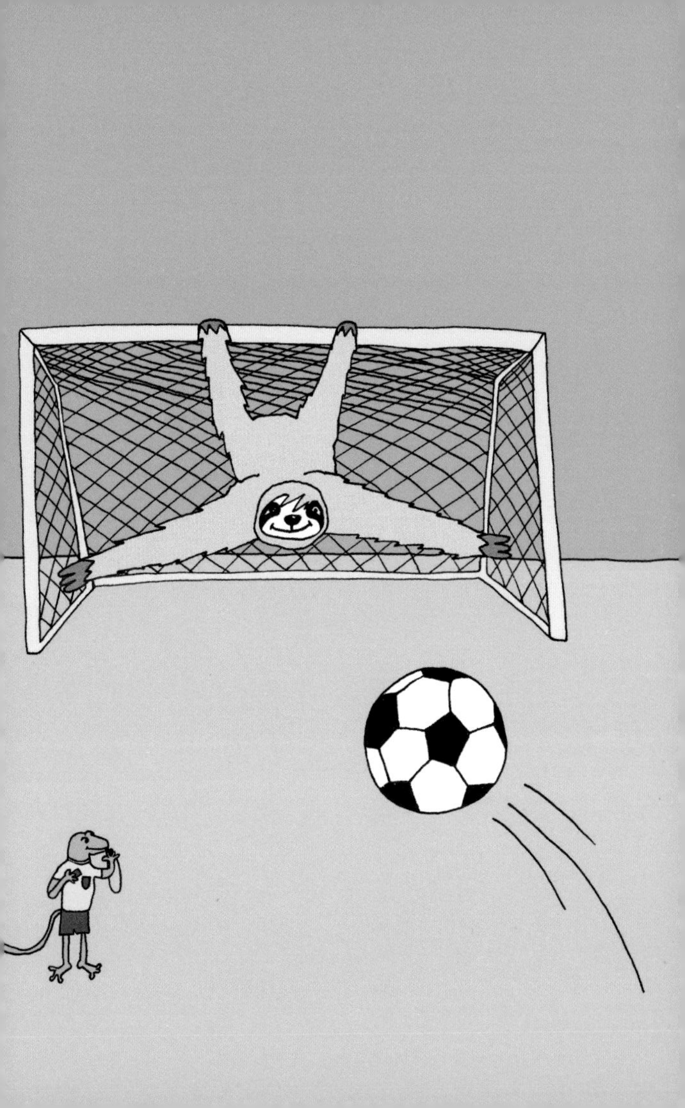

Quality not quantity,
thought Sloth.

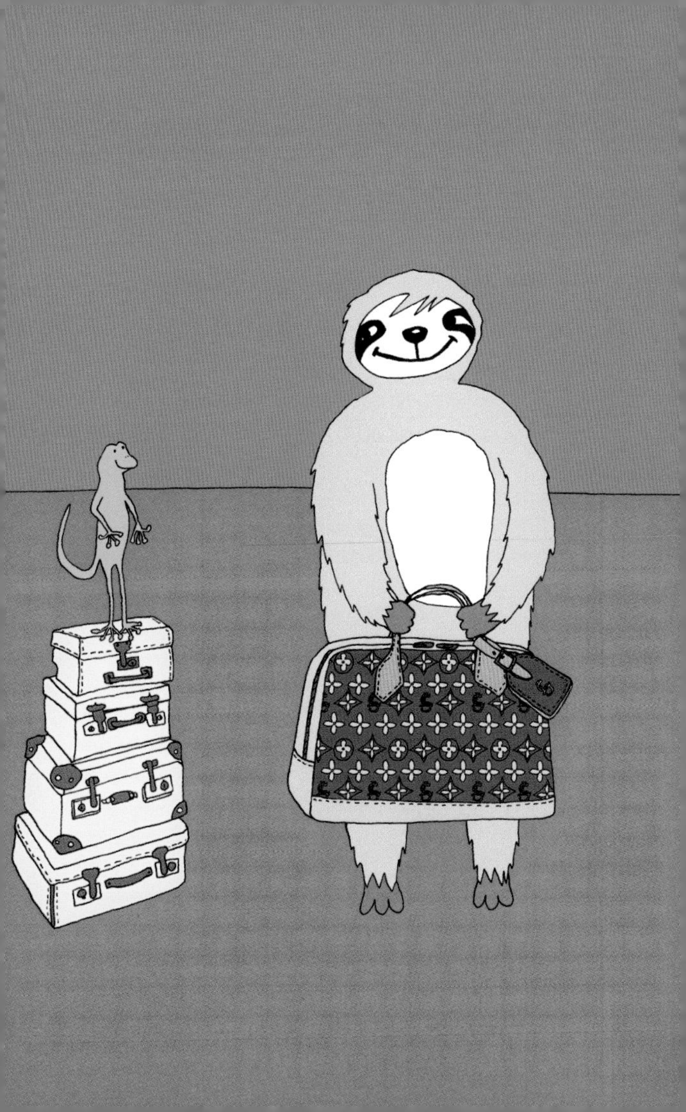

Sloth tried to look at things from all angles.

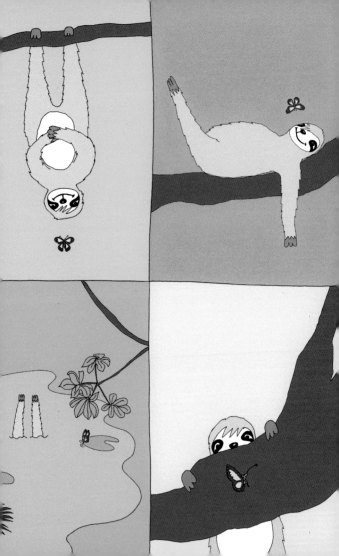

Sloth had decluttered
for a simpler life.

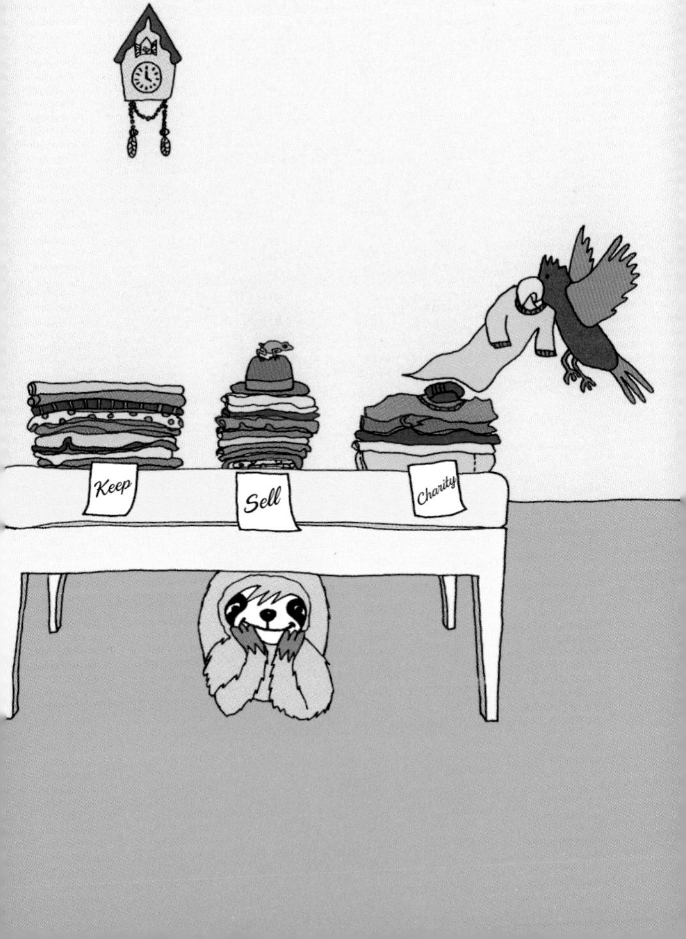
Keep
Sell
Charity

Sloth had turned
off his phone.

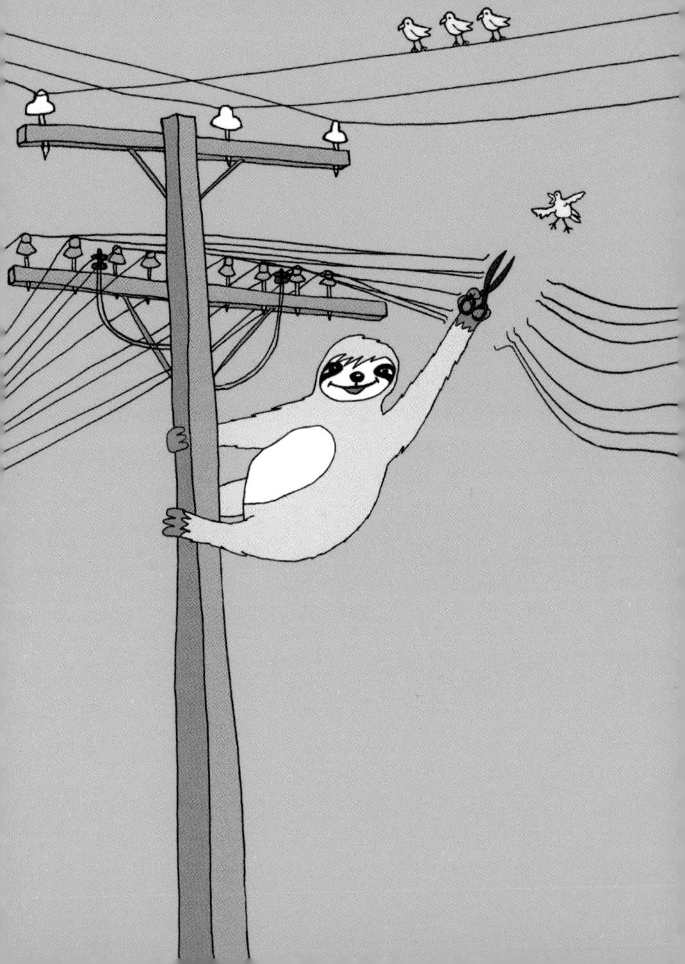

Sloth was keeping
himself current.

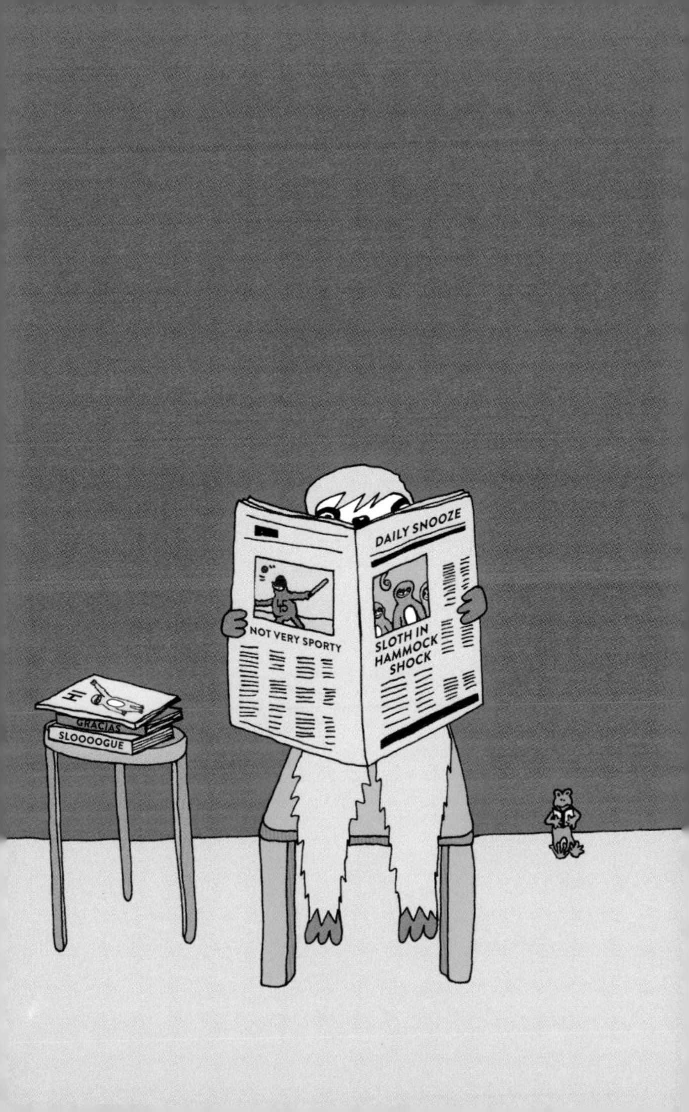
NOT VERY SPORTY
DAILY SNOOZE
SLOTH IN HAMMOCK SHOCK
GRACIAS
SLOOOOGUE

Sloth was eating
mindfully.

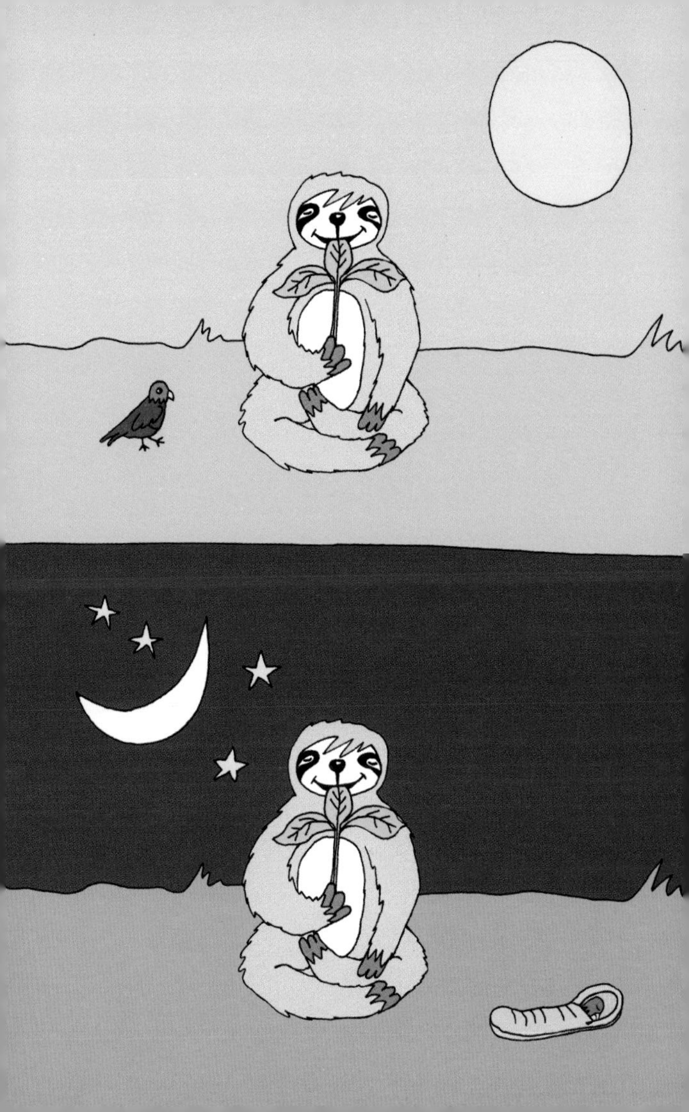

Sloth thought laughter
was the best medicine.

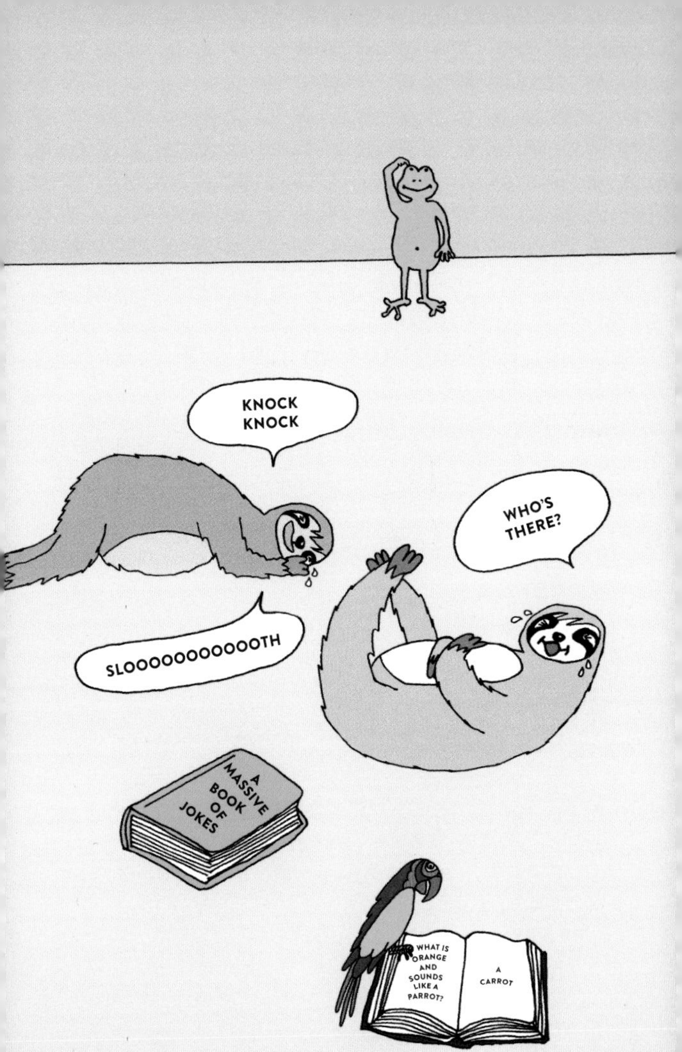
KNOCK KNOCK
WHO'S THERE?
SLOOOOOOOOOOOTH
A MASSIVE BOOK OF JOKES
WHAT IS ORANGE AND SOUNDS LIKE A PARROT?
A CARROT

Sloth knew when to
speak up and when
to be quiet.

Sloth got great pleasure
from small things.

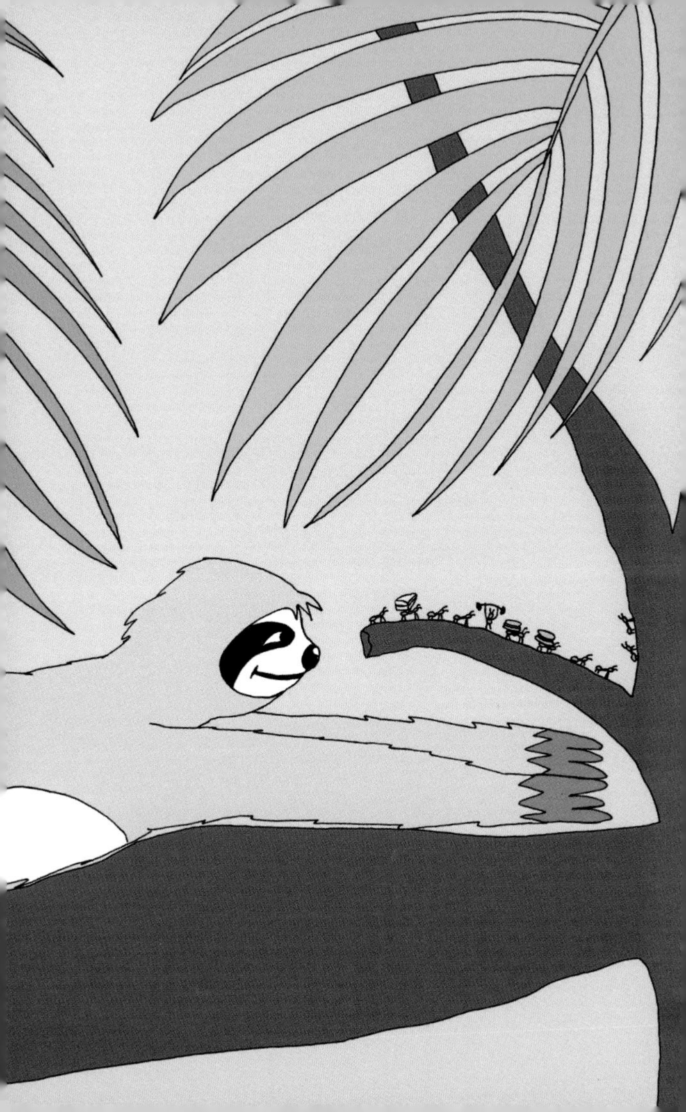

Sloth takes life at his
own pace – now go and
do the same.

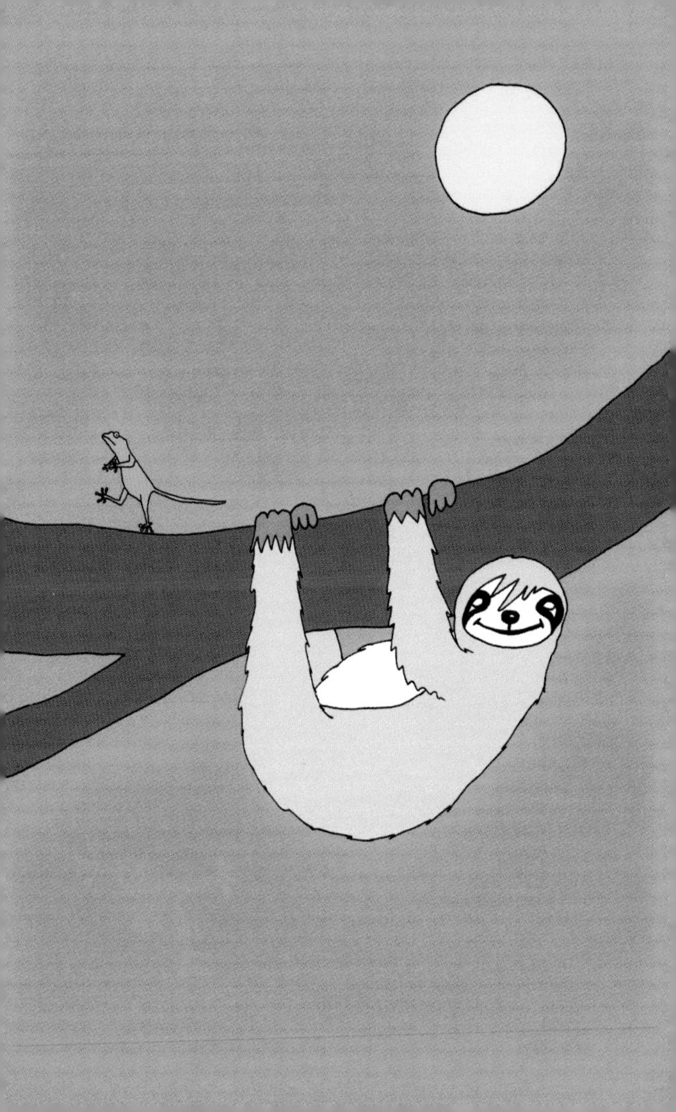

An Hachette UK Company
www.hachette.co.uk

First published in Great Britain
in 2018 by Spruce, an imprint of
Octopus Publishing Group Ltd
Carmelite House
50 Victoria Embankment
London EC4Y 0DZ
www.octopusbooks.co.uk

Distributed in the US by
Hachette Book Group
1290 Avenue of the Americas
4th and 5th Floors
New York, NY 10104

Distributed in Canada by
Canadian Manda Group
664 Annette St.
Toronto, Ontario, Canada M6S 2C8

Sarah Ford asserts the moral right
to be identified as the author of
this work.

ISBN 978-1-84601-578-6

A CIP catalogue record for this
book is available from the British
Library.

Printed and bound in Italy

10 9 8 7 6

Consultant Publisher
Sarah Ford

Assistant Editor
Ellie Corbett

Designer and Illustrator
Anita Mangan

Senior Designer
Jaz Bahra

Design Assistant
Robyn Shiner

Senior Production Manager
Peter Hunt

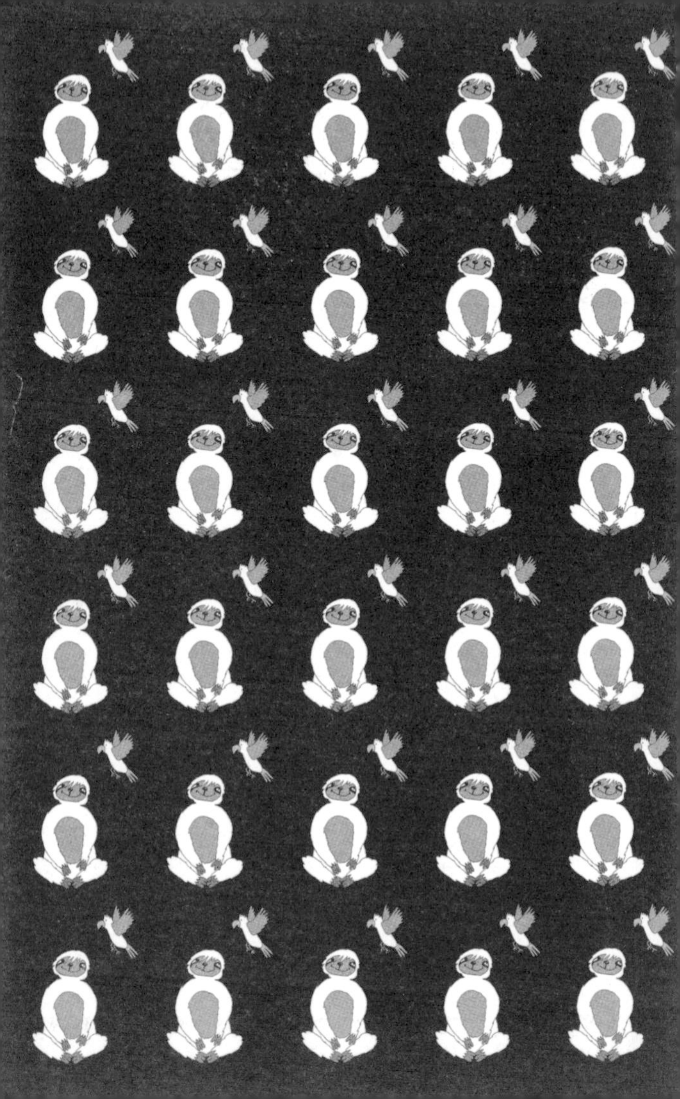